Exploring Music

EUNICE BOARDMAN • BETH LANDIS

SPECIAL CONSULTANTS

Barbara Andress
Buryl A. Red

HOLT, RINEHART AND WINSTON, INC.
New York, Toronto, London, Sydney

Consultants

Milton Babbitt

Keith E. Baird

Louis W. Ballard

Chou Wen-chung

Dorothy K. Gillett

Alan Lomax

Kurt Miller

Elena Paz

Virginia Stroh Red

Fela Sowande

Kurt Stone

Nelmatilda Woodard

Music autography by Maxwell Weaner

Illustrated by Robert J. Lee
  Sal Murdocca
  Melanie G. Arwin
  David Chestnutt

ISBN: 0-03-000086-6

5678 032 987654

Picture Sources

p. 5–Collection of Mr. & Mrs. Leo Castelli, New York; p. 40–Warren Ballard from DPI; p. 51–New York Public Library; p. 67–Swedish Information Center; p. 74–Susan Schiff from DPI; p. 124–Howard Byrne from DPI; p. 127–Tiers from Monkmeyer; p. 128–United Nations; p. 129–Herbert Lanks from Monkmeyer; p. 136–Novosti from Sovfoto; p. 140–Fred Ward from Black Star; p. 146–McGinnis from Monkmeyer; p. 147–South African Information Service; p. 156–Ema from DPI; p. 163–Grete Mannheim from DPI; p. 192–Bruce Frisch from Photo Researchers.

ACKNOWLEDGMENTS

Grateful acknowledgment is given to the following authors and publishers.

Bantam Books, Inc., for "Üsküdar" from *Folk Songs of the World*, copyright © 1966 by Charles Haywood. Used by permission.

Cooperative Recreation Service, Inc., for "Prayer for Africa" and "Nana Kru," from *African Songs*, copyright 1958; and "East Wind," from *A Sampler of Japanese Songs*, copyright 1958. Used by permission.

J. Curwen & Sons Limited for "The Purple Bamboo," from *Folksongs of China* and "Alleluia," English translation by W. H. Draper from *School Worship*. Used by permission.

The John Day Company Inc., for "Flower Drum Song," from *The Flower Drum and Other Chinese Songs* by Chin-Hsin Yao Chen and Shih-Hsiang, copyright 1943. Used by permission.

W. J. Gage Ltd., for "Who Can Sail?" from *Music for Young Canada*. Used by permission.

International Music Conference, sponsored by UNESCO, at Manila in 1966, for "Salidommay," from *Philippine Folk Dances and Songs*, edited by Dr. Grancisca R. Aquino, Superintendent of Physical Education of the Bureau of Public Schools. Used by permission.

MCA Music, a division of MCA, Inc. 445 Park Avenue, New York, N.Y. 10022, and Anglo Soviet Music Press, Ltd., for excerpt from *Symphony No. 5* by Dmitri Shostakovich, copyright 1945. All rights reserved. Used by permission.

Oak Publications for "Friend, Since You Want to Marry," from *Folksongs of Greece* by Susan and Ted Alevizos, © 1968 by Oak Publications. All rights reserved. Used by permission.

Oxford University Press for the English words by Jack Dobbs to "Migildi Magildi," from *The Oxford School Music Books*, copyright Oxford University Press, London; and Hughes A'l Fab for the melody, copyright by Hughes A'l Fab, Wrexham, North Wales. Used by permission.

Oxford University Press for "Ev'ry Night When the Sun Goes In," from *Folk Songs from the Southern Appalachians*, copyright 1917 by Oxford University Press, London. Used by permission.

M. Ring, 4 Sharnolds, Boughton Lane, Kent, England for "Hungarian Round" ("Evening Air") by Betty Askwith from the *Kent County Song Book*.

E. C. Schirmer Music Company for "The Silver Moon Is Shining." Reprinted with permission.

G. Schirmer, Inc., for "Manamolela" from *Choral Folksongs of the Bantu*, by Williams & Maselwa. English lyrics by Pete Seeger, copyright 1960 by G. Schirmer, Inc. Used by permission.

G. Schirmer for "The Home Road" by John Alden Carpenter, copyright by G. Schirmer, Inc. Used by permission.

Schocken Books for "Tum Balalyka," from *A Treasury of Jewish Folksongs* by Ruth Rubin, copyright 1950 by Schocken Books, Inc. New York. Used by permission.

Walton Music Corporation for "Softly Calls the Cuckoo," from *Songs of Man* by Luboff & Stracke. Used by permission.

Additional copyright acknowledgments and photo credits appear with the materials used.

Contents

Let's Explore Music

Music can be a lifetime exploration! As you explore the many paths that lead to the enjoyment of music, you will discover that each path has some interesting branches to follow.

You can discover musical sounds produced by voices, instruments, and electronic devices. You can explore various ways the sound is organized. You can listen to music written by composers of the past and present. You can learn folk music of many times and places.

You can explore music as a means of personal expression. You can express your own thoughts and feelings with music. Often, you can discover something about the feelings of others from their music.

As you explore the sounds of music, its literature, and its expressive qualities, you will discover that it is an important part of life for many people. Think about your own community. When and where can music be heard? What types of music are available? Do you know people who have jobs dealing with music? Do you know others who enjoy music as a hobby? As you sing and play music, dance and listen to music, you will find a place for yourself in this musical world.

America, the Beautiful

Music by Samuel A. Ward
Words by Katharine Lee Bates

The song on this page and the one on page 4 were composed by Americans who expressed their feelings about this country through music.

During the school year you will be studying the music of other countries. Look for examples of patriotic songs from these lands. Compare the songs with those of your own country.

1. O beau - ti - ful for spa - cious skies,
2. O beau - ti - ful for pil - grim feet
3. O beau - ti - ful for he - roes proved

For am - ber waves of grain,
Whose stern, im - pas - sioned stress
In lib - er - at - ing strife,

For pur - ple moun - tain maj - es - ties
A thor - ough - fare for free - dom beat
Who more than self their coun - try loved,

A - bove the fruit - ed plain!
A - cross the wil - der - ness!
And mer - cy more than life!

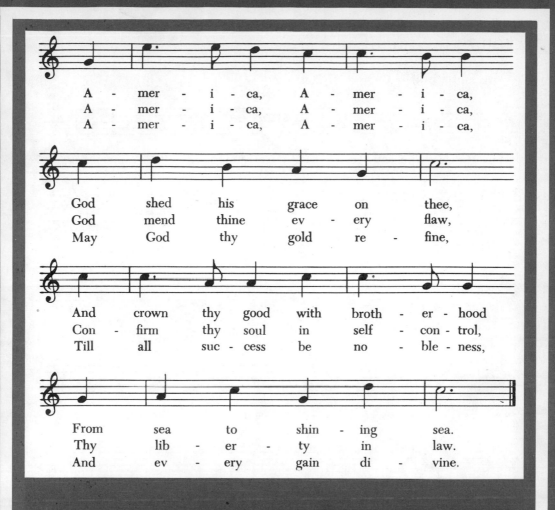

A - mer - i - ca,   A - mer - i - ca,
A - mer - i - ca,   A - mer - i - ca,
A - mer - i - ca,   A - mer - i - ca,

God   shed   his   grace   on   thee,
God   mend   thine   ev - ery   flaw,
May   God   thy   gold   re - fine,

And   crown   thy   good   with   broth - er - hood
Con - firm   thy   soul   in   self - con - trol,
Till   all   suc - cess   be   no - ble - ness,

From   sea   to   shin - ing   sea.
Thy   lib - er - ty   in   law.
And   ev - ery   gain   di - vine.

Sing this descant with the refrain.

A - mer - i - ca,   A - mer - i - ca, _____ A -

mer - i - ca,   A - mer - i - ca.

You're a Grand Old Flag

Words and Music by George M. Cohan

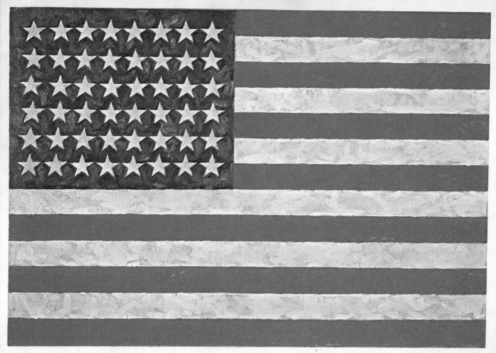

Flag, Jasper Johns, 1958

American Salute

by Morton Gould

You have learned many songs written by composers which show pride in their country. Other composers have taken American themes and written instrumental compositions. Morton Gould has taken a familiar marching tune from the Civil War and used it as the basis for his music. Listen to the beginning of the composition. The introduction uses fragments of the theme. Then it is stated in its entirety by the bassoons. How quickly can you identify the tune? You may have learned to sing it in fifth grade.

Morton Gould developed many variations around this theme. You have heard other compositions based on **theme and variations**. Review what you know about this form. Make a list of the different ways you have heard composers vary themes.

Listen to "American Salute." How many of the ways you listed did you hear in Gould's music? Did he include any variations that you had not listed?

Choose a favorite American song and develop your own variations. Use some of the ideas you heard in the music by Morton Gould.

5

Roll On, Columbia

Words and Music by Woody Guthrie

This song of the Northwest might be called a "composed folk song." Compare the musical style with that of "America, the Beautiful" and "You're a Grand Old Flag." All three express feelings about America. Why is only "Roll On, Columbia" considered a folk song?

1. Green Doug - las fir where the wa - ters cut through,
2. Oth - er great riv - ers add pow - er to you,
3. Tom Jef - fer - son's vi - sion would not let him rest;

Down her wild moun - tains and can - yons she flew,
Yak - i - ma, Snake, and the Klick - i - tat, too,
An em - pire he saw in the Pa - cif - ic North - west;

Ca - nad - ian North - west to the o - cean so blue;
Sand - y Wil - lam - ette and Hood Riv - er, too;
Sent Lew - is and Clark ___ and they did the rest;

Roll on, Co - lum - bia, roll on! _____

Refrain

Roll on, roll on, _____

(Melody)

Roll on, Co - lum - bia, roll on!

4. At Bonneville now there are ships in the locks;
   The waters have risen and cleared all the rocks.
   Shiploads of plenty will steam past the docks;
   Roll on, Columbia, roll on!
   Refrain

5. And on up the river is Grand Coulee Dam,
   The mightiest thing ever built by a man,
   To run the great fact'ries and water the land;
   Roll on, Columbia, roll on!
   Refrain

Sunny Day

Words and Music by Donovan Leitch

How do you know this is a song of your own time? The rhythm of this song is interesting because it is constantly changing. Practice these patterns before you learn the song.

Sun-ny Day   while a - way the af - ter- noon

Cut - ting net - tles that are hid - ing pet - als pink

From the riv - er   drink.   Blue - bells

wood   dells where dwells a   squir - rel   who   slinks a -

long   branched pat - terns height-ens call   of coal - tit small

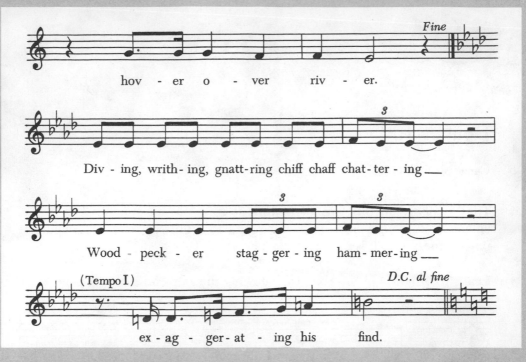

hov - er o - ver riv - er.

Div - ing, writh - ing, gnatt- ring chiff chaff chat - ter - ing __

Wood - peck - er stag - ger - ing ham - mer - ing __

ex - ag - ger- at - ing his find.

Music for Electric Guitar

Geordie

Old English Folk Song

This performance of "Geordie" by The New York Electric String Ensemble features the electric guitar. The sound of the music is contemporary, but the guitar is an ancient instrument. Of Oriental origin, it has become popular in almost every country of the world. Folk singers use it to accompany themselves; popular performing groups of today may use several different types. Even classical composers have written music for the guitar.

Through the centuries, the guitar has undergone many changes in shape, size, number of strings, and so on. The most recent change has been the development of the electric guitar, which magnifies the sound electronically.

The melody of "Geordie" is based on an old English folk song. Why does the music sound new?

Donkey Riding

Canadian Folk Song

The "donkey" in this Canadian work song is not an animal. It is a small engine used around docks to haul cargo. The engine has less than one horse-power, therefore, it is called a "donkey."

Learn the rhythm of this song by following the steps on the next page.

1. Were you ev - er in Que - bec, Stow - ing tim - ber
2. Were you ev - er in Car - diff Bay, Where the folks all

on a deck, Where there's a king with a
shout "Hoo - ray! Here comes — John with his

gold - en crown, Rid - ing on a don - key?
three months' pay, Rid - ing on a don - key."

Refrain

Hey - ho! A - way we go! Don - key rid - ing, don - key rid - ing,

Hey - ho! A - way we go, Rid - ing on a don - key!

10

Exploring
Rhythmic Notation

When learning the rhythm of a new song from notation, you must complete certain steps. How many of these can you complete as you learn the songs on pages 10 and 12?

- Determine the **meter**. That is, decide whether the **beats** are grouped by **accents** in twos, threes, or some other combination.

  Look at the **upper number** of the **meter signature**.
  Notice how the notes are grouped within the **measures**.

- Discover the note which will sound with the beat.

  Look at the **lower number** of the meter signature.

  $2 = \half$ $4 = \quarter$ $8 = \eighth$

  Can you think of another way to discover the note that sounds with the **beat**?

- Study the rhythm of the melody.

  Find patterns which include notes that sound with the beat.
  Find patterns which include notes that are **longer** than the beat.
  Find patterns which include notes that are **shorter** than the beat.

  Look for rhythm patterns that are repeated.
  Look for unusual rhythm patterns.

- Establish the meter.

  Clap the beat lightly, or tap a percussion instrument.
  Accent the first beat in each group of notes.

- Practice the unusual rhythm patterns.

- Practice the rhythm of the complete song.

  Play the rhythm on an instrument.
  Clap it.
  Chant the words.

- Now you are ready to learn the melody.

11

Acres of Clams

Canadian Folk Song

Follow the steps on page 11 and read the rhythm. In what ways were your answers different from those discovered when you studied the rhythm of "Donkey Riding"? Were any answers the same?

What must you do when you see the **tie?** ⌒   If you are not sure, listen to the recording. Tap the beat and listen to the melody. Can you decide why the tie is used?

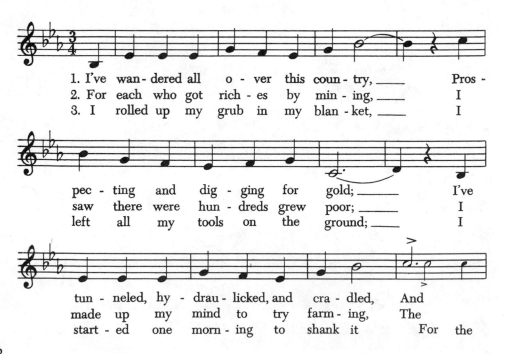

1. I've wan - dered all   o - ver   this coun - try, _____   Pros -
2. For each who got   rich - es   by   min - ing, _____   I
3. I   rolled up   my   grub   in   my   blan - ket, _____   I

pec - ting   and   dig - ging   for   gold; _____   I've
saw   there   were   hun - dreds   grew   poor; _____   I
left   all   my   tools   on   the   ground; _____   I

tun - neled, hy - drau - licked, and   cra - dled,   And
made   up   my   mind   to   try   farm - ing,   The
start - ed   one   morn - ing   to   shank   it   For the

I have been fre - quent - ly sold, _____ And
on - ly pur - suit that is sure, _____ The
coun - try they call Pu - get Sound, _____ For the

I have been fre - quent - ly sold, _____ And
on - ly pur - suit that is sure, _____ The
coun - try they call Pu - get Sound, _____ For the

I have been fre - quent - ly sold. _____ I've
on - ly pur - suit that is sure. _____ I
coun - try they call Pu - get Sound. _____ I

tun - neled, hy - drau - licked, and cra - dled, And
made up my mind to try farm - ing, The
start - ed one morn - ing to shank it For the

I have been fre - quent - ly sold. _____
on - ly pur - suit that is sure. _____
coun - try they call Pu - get Sound. _____

4. No longer the slave of ambition,
   I laugh at the world and its shams;
   And think of my happy condition
   Surrounded by acres of clams.
   Surrounded by acres of clams,
   Surrounded by acres of clams.
   And think of my happy condition
   Surrounded by acres of clams.

In Bahía

Brazilian Folk Song
Words Adapted

Follow the steps on page 11 as you learn this Brazilian samba. When you reach step three, be sure to notice the unusual rhythm pattern in measure one. Practice this **syncopated** pattern. In what way is it unusual?

La la la la la la la la la la la la la la la la

La la la la la la la la la la la la la

1. In Ba - hí - a town, far a - way,
2. In Ba - hí - a town, if you wish,

Co - co - nuts are eas - y to buy, five cents is all you pay.
Salt - ed pea-nuts you may buy there for just ten cents a dish.

14

When you know the song, study the rhythms of the accompaniment. Learn to play each pattern. Then some people may play the accompaniment while others sing.

As the Sun Goes Down

Words and Music by Josef Marais

Determine the scale on which this song is based by studying the melody of the first three lines. Put the different notes in order from low to high on the staff. Play them on the bells.

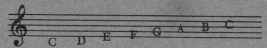

The pattern you played is the **C major scale.** This song is based on that scale; that is, the tones of the melody are from that scale. The song is in the **key of C.** Sing 1 3 5 8. Sing the song with numbers.

Play the C scale on the bells. Describe the sequence you played. Use the term **half step** when you hear the tones that are closest together. Use **whole step** for the distance between all other tones in the scale.

Follow the sequence of whole and half steps which you discovered in the C scale, and play scales beginning on F, E♭, G, and D.

For each scale, give the number of the steps where it was necessary to play black bells (sharps or flats) in order to fill the sequence of whole and half steps.

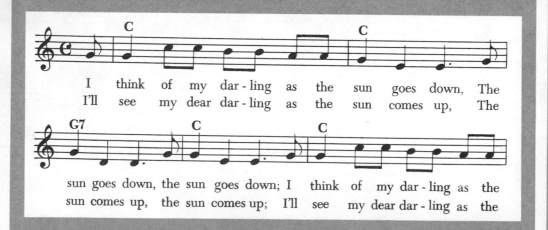

I think of my dar-ling as the sun goes down, The
I'll see my dear dar-ling as the sun comes up, The

sun goes down, the sun goes down; I think of my dar-ling as the
sun comes up, the sun comes up; I'll see my dear dar-ling as the

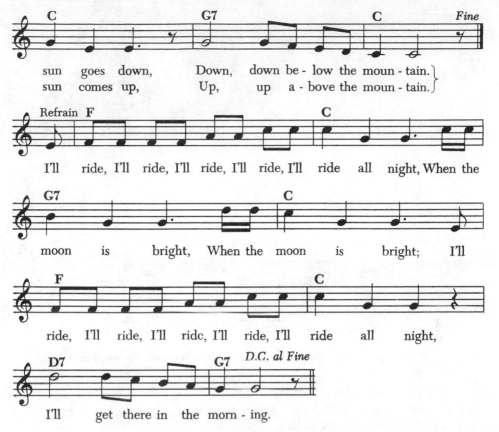

sun goes down, Down, down be-low the moun-tain.
sun comes up, Up, up a-bove the moun-tain.

Refrain F

I'll ride, I'll ride, I'll ride, I'll ride, I'll ride all night, When the

G7   C

moon is bright, When the moon is bright; I'll

F   C

ride, I'll ride, I'll ride, I'll ride, I'll ride all night,

D7   G7   *D.C. al Fine*

I'll get there in the morn-ing.

Come to the Land

Romanian Folk Song

Here are two scales. One is **major,** the other is **minor.** Play the two scales. You know the sequence of whole and half steps for the major scale. Now determine the sequence for the minor scale.

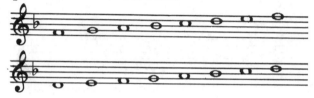

"Come to the Land" is based on one of these scales. "Streets of Laredo" is based on the other. To decide which scale belongs to each song, study the melodies. Songs usually center around steps 1, 3, and 5. Which song centers around steps 1, 3, and 5 of the D minor scale? Which song centers around those steps of the F major scale?

When you have determined the scale for each song, learn it by singing the pitch numbers.

Come to the land with joy and with spir - it,

Come to our na - tive land; We have plowed the

fields and have plant-ed grain, We'll reap a might-y har - vest.

Streets of Laredo

Cowboy Song

| F | C7 | F | C7 |

1. As I _____ walked out in the streets of La - re - do,
2. "I see by your out - fit that you are a cow - boy,"
3. "Get six jol - ly cow - boys to car - ry my cof - fin,
4. "Oh, beat the drum slow - ly and play the fife low - ly,

| F | C7 | F | C7 |

As I _____ walked out in La - re - do one day,
These words he did say as I bold - ly walked by;
Get six pur - ty maid - ens to sing me a song;
Play the dead march as you car - ry me a long;

| F | C7 | F | C7 |

I spied a young cow - boy all wrapped in white lin - en,
"Come sit down be - side me and hear my sad sto - ry,
Take me to the val - ley and lay the sod o'er me,
Put bunch - es of ros - es all o - ver my cof - fin,

| F | Gm | C7 | F |

All wrapped in white lin - en and cold as the clay.
I'm shot in the breast and I know I must die."
For I'm a young cow - boy and know I've done wrong."
Ros - es to dead - en the clods as they fall."

19

Ev'ry Night When the Sun Goes In

Southern Folk Song
Arranged by
William S. Haynie

1. Ev - 'ry night
2. Love, don't weep,

(Melody)

1. Ev - 'ry night _____ when the sun goes
weep, _____ true _ love, don't

when the sun goes in, Ev - 'ry
true _ love, don't mourn, Love, don't

in, _____ Ev - 'ry night _____
mourn, _____ True love, don't weep, _____

night   when the sun goes in,
weep,   true __ love, don't mourn,

__ when the sun goes in, _____ Ev - 'ry
__ true __ love, don't mourn, _____ True love, don't

Ev - 'ry   night   when the sun goes
Love,   don't weep   nor __ mourn for

night _____ when the sun goes in, _____
weep _____ nor __ mourn for me, _____

in,   Hang   my   head
me,   Goin'   a -   way

__ I   hang down my head _____ and mourn - ful
__ I'm go - ing a - way _____ to   Mar - ble -

and   mourn - ful   cry.   town.
to   Mar - ble -

cry. _____ 2. True love, don't
town. _____

21

Exploring Melodic Notation

To learn a new song from notation, begin by studying the words and discussing the meaning of the song. Next, learn the rhythm. Then learn the melody by following these steps.

- Determine **home tone**. Home tone is always step 1 of the scale. Begin by studying the **key signature.**

  Is it in sharps? The **last sharp** will be the **seventh step** of the scale. How will you find home tone?

  Is the key signature in flats? The **last flat** will be the **fourth step** of the scale. How will you find home tone?

  Check your answer by studying the tones of the melody. A song usually centers around 1 3 5 of the scale. Does the song often return to these tones?

- Study the melodic notation.

  Look for melody patterns that include scale steps.
  Look for patterns based on tones of the I chord (1 3 5).
  Look for patterns based on tones from the V chord (5 7 2).
  Look for wide skips or unusual intervals.

- Establish the sound of the key.

  Play 1 3 5 8 on the bells or piano.
  Play I IV V7 I on the autoharp or piano.
  Sing 1 3 5 8 5 3 1.

- Practice singing and playing difficult or unusual melody patterns.

- Sing the melody with numbers, on a neutral syllable such as "loo," or with words.

- When you are sure of the melody, practice until you can sing the song with appropriate dynamics and tempo.

Viva, viva la musica

Words and Music by Michael Praetorius

Follow the instructions on page 22 as you learn the melody. Then sing the song as a round.

Vi - va, vi - va la mu - si - ca,

Vi - va, vi - va la mu - si - ca,

Vi - va la mu - si - ca!

Kyrie

Traditional Round

Are there any similarities between this song and "Viva, viva la musica"? The Latin words, *"Kyrie eleison,"* mean "Lord, have mercy."

Ky - ri - e, Ky - ri - e e - lei - son.

Ky - ri - e, Ky - ri - e e - lei - son.

Ky - ri - e, Ky - ri - e____ e - lei - son.

He's Got the Whole World in His Hands

Spiritual

1. He's got the whole world___ in his hands,__ He's got the
2. He's got the wind and rain___ in his hands,__ He's got the
3. He's got both you and me ___ in his hands,__ He's got both

whole world___ in his hands,__ He's got the whole world ___
wind and rain ___ in his hands,__ He's got the wind and rain ___
you and me ___ in his hands,__ He's got both you and me ___

in his hands,_ He's got the whole world in his hands. __
in his hands,_ He's got the whole world in his hands. __
in his hands,_ He's got the whole world in his hands. __

One group may sing this chant while another group sings the melody. Listen to the interesting harmony created by the two voices.

He's got the whole wide world ___ in his hands, He's got the

whole wide world in his hands, He's got the whole wide world ___

in his hands, He's got the whole world in his hands. ___

William Tell Overture

by Gioacchino Rossini

Many people know the dramatic story of William Tell, a courageous Swiss patriot who lived during the fourteenth century. Review the story of how and why he shot an apple off his son's head. Lovers of freedom have long found meaning in the story. The opera *William Tell* is based on it.

Although the overture was originally composed to open the opera, it is often heard today as a separate concert piece. The overture is in four parts.

At Dawn

The first section suggests sunrise in the Swiss Alps. It begins with a beautiful, quiet passage. Why do you think the composer chose the cellos to play this section? What else helps us imagine the peaceful scene?

The Storm

The strings and woodwinds give warning that the scene is changing, and the storm breaks quickly and furiously through the orchestra. What happens in the music to build the excitement of the storm?

The Calm

This **pastorale** suggests the peacefulness of the land and of the shepherd's life. It begins with a shepherd song. Which instruments imitate the sound of the Alpine horn and its echo through the mountains?

Finale

The tranquil scene is interrupted by the fanfare of trumpets which begins a stirring march. This familiar march moves so fast that it is more like a gallop. Then the overture closes brilliantly with a **coda.**

As you listen to each section, discuss these questions. What musical devices does the composer use to paint each picture? Which element of music—rhythm, melody, harmony—seems to you to be the most important in each section? How does the composer create the four contrasting moods?

Using this composition as an example, what do you think is meant by the term **"program music"**?

The Swan

Traditional Round

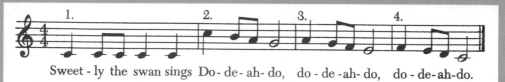

Sing this round in four parts. As you sing, listen to the interesting harmony created by your voices. Notice how the tones combine to create **chords.**

Chords can be built on any tone of the scale. In traditional songs, the chords in the harmony usually are built in intervals of **thirds.**

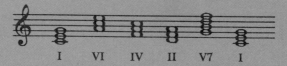

Play and sing each chord. Notice the differences in **quality** of sound. Play the tones of each chord one after another. Can you decide why they have different qualities? Which chords are **major?** Which are **minor?**

Chords can also be built with other intervals. Sing this pattern as a three-part round. When all three parts are sounding, you hear chords made up of **fourths.**

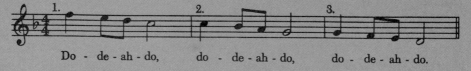

Sing this pattern as a round. What interval makes up the chords you are singing now?

A Hundred Years Ago

American Windlass Song

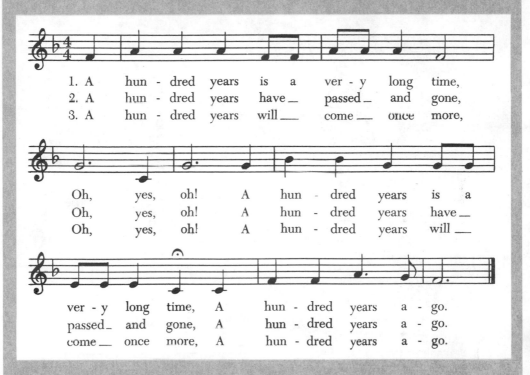

1. A hun - dred years is a ver - y long time,
2. A hun - dred years have ___ passed ___ and gone,
3. A hun - dred years will ___ come ___ once more,

Oh, yes, oh! A hun - dred years is a
Oh, yes, oh! A hun - dred years have ___
Oh, yes, oh! A hun - dred years will ___

ver - y long time, A hun - dred years a - go.
passed ___ and gone, A hun - dred years a - go.
come ___ once more, A hun - dred years a - go.

Add your own harmony to this song by following these steps.

1. Write out chords I VI IV II V7 I in the key of the song.

2. Study the melody, measure by measure. For each measure, select the chords from the ones you have written that include tones of the melody.

3. Play your chord sequence on the autoharp as you sing the melody. Did you like your choices? Experiment with other sequences.

You may add harmony to many songs by following the same steps.

Green Grow the Laurels

American Folk Song

1. Oo_____
2. Green _____ grow the lau - rels

(Melody)

1. I once had a sweet-heart but now I have none.
2. Oh, green grow the lau - rels all wet with the dew,

oo _____
Wet with dew, _____

He's gone and left me; I live all a - lone. I
Sad from the time that I part - ed from you. The

oo ———————
Hope ———— you'll prove true, ————

live   all   a - lone   and   con - tent - ed   I'll   be,   For
next   time   I   see   you   I   hope you'll prove true,   And

oo ————————————————
Change   to   red,   white   and   blue.

he   loves an - oth - er   one   bet - ter   than   me.
change   the   green   lau - rels   to   red,   white   and   blue.

Follow the steps given on page 27, and determine the chords to accompany
this song. Study the notes of both the melody and the descant as you decide
on a sequence of chords.

Play the accompaniment on the autoharp as the class sings.

Add a third harmony part to sing below the melody. Choose tones from the
chord sequence you played on the autoharp. It might begin like this.

DANCE & MUSIC

Expression in music and expression in dance have always gone hand in hand. In some parts of the world dance plays a part in ancient rituals and ceremonies. People have developed many dance forms for recreation—the minuet, the polka, the waltz, the square dance. Other types of dancing such as the ballet have been developed purely as art forms.

Dance is usually accompanied by music. Often you can guess the style and form of the dance by listening to the music. Listen to "Kalvelis," or "Little Blacksmith." How many parts do you hear? What kind of dance figures might be used?

The second composition is a **farandole.** The farandole is a very old dance from southern France. Everyone joins hands in one long line and follows the leader. This farandole by the French composer Bizet suggests the traditional dance music. You may enjoy developing a "follow-the-leader" dance. Use movements which reflect the melodies and rhythms you hear.

Look through your book. Find other dance music. Discuss the style of each example. What modern dances do you know? Does the music of these dances suggest the type of dance movements you use?

SH-MO
An Event for Four or Forty

Work in small groups to perform this composition. There must be at least five people in a group. Four are performers. One is the conductor. The key below the score will help you understand the notation used. Experiment with different arrangements that will result in interesting rhythms, contrasts of pitch levels, texture, intensity, dynamics, and tone color.

ONE	/////////	/\/\/\/\/	☐ X SH ∿∿	MO ↗ / MO ↘
TWO	☐	WH ∿∿——	/////////	↗↗↗ SH∿∿ / MO MO MO
THREE	XXXX SH∿∿	XXXX XXXX	☐ /\	MO ↗ MO ↗ / MO ↓ MO ↘
FOUR	☐	WH ∿∿——	SH ∿∿ ↗↗ / MO MO	↗↗ / MO MO WH∿∿——

////// = tongue clicks

/\/\/\/\ = shuffling feet

X = loud clap

☐ = silence

SH ∿∿∿∿ = shushing sound

WH ∿∿—— = three words, whispered but distinct, repeated over and over (words are selected by each performer)

MO = moaning or wailing sound (arrow indicates rising or falling pitch levels)

Each sound continues until the end of the section, or part of the section, as indicated by the score. Each of the four sections in the score should last about 30 seconds. The conductor gives the cue for the performance to begin and also indicates when each new section begins.

SOUNDS of COUNTRY

Have you ever listened to a recording of country music and wondered how the performers achieve their special "country" sound? Here is the vocal line for a "country" version of "He's Got the Whole World in His Hands."

Easy country shuffle

He's got the whole world — in his hands, — He's got the

whole world — in his hands, — He's got the whole world —

in his hands, — He's got the whole world in his hands.

Now review the version you learned on page 24. How was the rhythm of the song changed in the country version? Listen to the harmony part in the country version. How is it different from harmony parts in most songs you know?

You can create your own country arrangement. First learn to sing the country version of the song. Then choose from these patterns and plan a combination of sounds that gives the effect you want.

AUTOHARP: Play the chords in this rhythm. Let the sound ring.

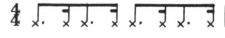

PIANO: Play "fills." Insert them wherever you see a half note.

for C chords   for G7 chords

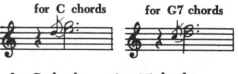

BELLS: Play these sounds with soft mallets to get a vibe-like effect.

for C chords   for G7 chords

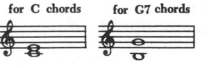

32

In the "country" version, the entire rhythm of the melody was changed. You can suggest a "soul" feeling by singing the original rhythm of the melody and adding a harmony part. Sing the melody with a smooth, heavy sound and a steady beat.

(He's got the   whole) Whole world __   Oo.   Whole world __   Oo.

Whole   world __   Oo.   World   in   his   hands.

Now choose a "lead" singer to sing the melody as a solo, and let the harmony singers serve as a "back-up" group. Does your song sound more like soul music now?

If you have heard much soul music, you probably know that hand-clapping plays an important part in achieving the soul sound. Try adding any of these clapping patterns to your song.

Instrumental parts

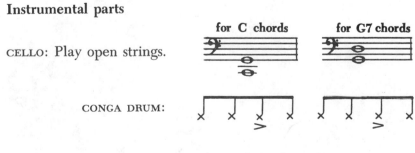

CELLO: Play open strings.

for C chords   for G7 chords

CONGA DRUM:

AUTOHARP:

33

Music of the British Isles and Scandinavia

The British Isles include England, Scotland, Ireland, and Wales. The region known as Scandinavia includes Norway, Denmark, Sweden, and Iceland. Locate each country on the map and talk about its geography and climate. What do you know about its history? Think about how these factors might have affected the music of each country.

Composers from the British Isles and Scandinavia have written music that is known all over the world. In this unit you will study music written in England four hundred years ago, as well as the music of modern British composers. You will also hear the music of Edvard Grieg, a Norwegian composer who lived during the nineteenth century.

Compare the musical styles of the different countries. How is the music of a particular country distinctive? Discover some of the folk instruments of these regions, such as the Irish harp, the Scottish bagpipe, and the Norwegian fiddle.

In the art section of your book are works of art from the British Isles and Scandinavia. As you study musical styles, notice the characteristics of the visual art of these lands.

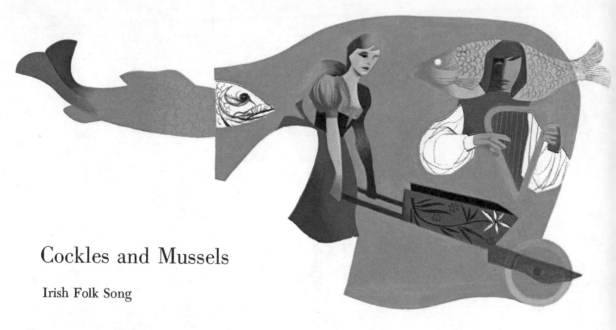

Cockles and Mussels

Irish Folk Song

Liltingly

1. In Dub - lin's fair cit - y, where girls are so pret - ty,
2. She was a fish - mon - ger, but sure 'twas no won - der,
3. She died of a fe - ver and no one could save her,

I first set me eyes on sweet Mol - ly Ma - lone,
For so were her fa - ther and moth - er be - fore;
And that was the end of sweet Mol - ly Ma - lone;

As she wheeled her wheel - bar - row through streets broad and nar - row,
And they wheeled their wheel - bar - row through streets broad and nar - row,
Now her ghost wheels her bar - row through streets broad and nar - row,

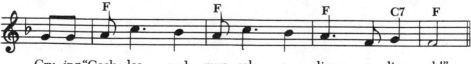

Cry - ing, "Cock - les and mus - sels, a - live, a - live oh!"

Listen to the recording. Notice the harp accompaniment. Irish minstrels often accompanied themselves on the harp as they sang. Many times the harp was a young man's most prized possession. He carried it to war with him and, if he was killed, his harp was buried with him. The harp is so important to the Irish people that it is included as one of the emblems on their flag.

Many Irish ballads tell stories of the history of this proud people who fought long for freedom. There are also many love songs and songs of Irish folklore.

The Irish music we know today comes primarily from the seventeenth century, after Ireland had been defeated by England and English was the official language of the country. Versions of Irish songs such as "Cockles and Mussels" often are found in England and Scotland. Why would this be so?

When you have learned to sing this Irish ballad in two parts, play a harp-like accompaniment. You can suggest the sound of the harp by stroking the strings of the autoharp slowly.

The harmonizing part may be sung, or it may be played an octave higher on the flute or violin.

Johnny Has Gone for a Soldier

American Folk Song

Why do you think an American folk song is included with the music of Ireland? Listen to your recording and discuss reasons why. You will hear two versions of this song. The first, "Shule Aroon," was sung during the early eighteenth century when the Irish were fighting for freedom from the English. The second version was sung during the American Revolutionary War.

In what ways are the two versions similar? How are they different? Discuss the words and music.

1. There I sat on But-ter-milk Hill.
2. Me oh my, I loved him so;

Who could blame me, cry my fill? And
Broke my heart to see him go, And

ev-ery tear would turn a mill;
on-ly time will heal my woe;

John-ny has gone for a sol - dier.
John-ny has gone for a sol - dier.

Comin' Thro' the Rye

Old Scottish Air
Traditional adaptation
of a poem by Robert Burns

Follow the instructions on page 11, and learn the rhythm of this song. Then study the key signature. Look at the notes of the melody. On what kind of scale is this song based?

To help you decide, put the different pitches of the song in order from low to high. Play the pattern you created. Do you recognize the scale on which this pattern is based? Are any pitches missing in the scale?

1. If a bod-y meet a bod-y, Com-in' thro' the rye,
2. If a bod-y meet a bod-y, Com-in' frae the town,
3. A-mang the train there is a swain I dear-ly love my-sel', But

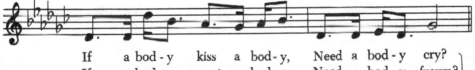

If a bod-y kiss a bod-y, Need a bod-y cry?
If a bod-y greet a bod-y, Need a bod-y frown?
what's his name or where's his hame, I din-na choose to tell.

Refrain

Ev-ery lass-ie has her lad-die, Nane they say ha'e_ I;

Yet a' the lads they smile on me, When com-in' thro' the rye.

Turn Ye to Me

Scottish Folk Song
Words by John Wilson

Study the design of this beautiful Scottish melody. How many phrases do you find? Are any exactly alike? Notice the slight changes in the melody which add interest.

With feeling

1. The stars are shin - ing cheer - i - ly, cheer - i - ly,
2. The waves are danc - ing mer - ri - ly, mer - ri - ly,

Ho - ro, Mhai - ri dhu, Turn ye _____ to me.
Ho - ro, Mhai - ri dhu, Turn ye _____ to me.

The sea - mew is moan - ing drea - ri - ly, drea - ri - ly,
The sea - birds are wail - ing wea - ri - ly, drea - ri - ly,

Ho - ro, Mhai - ri dhu, Turn ye _____ to me.
Ho - ro, Mhai - ri dhu, Turn ye _____ to me.

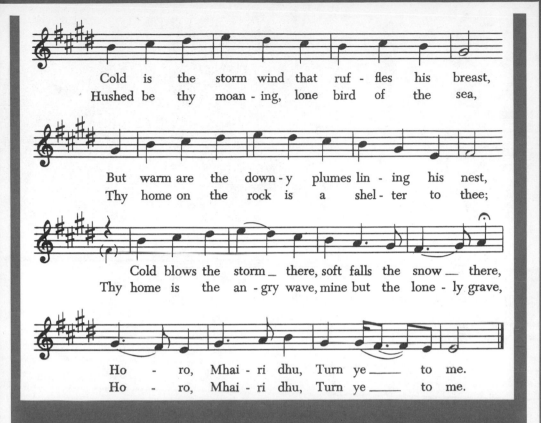

The music of Scotland is as varied as the terrain of the country. The songs from the Highlands are often highly expressive with wandering melodies that may change from major to minor within a single measure. The melodies from the Lowlands may be either slow and tender or sparkling and gay. The "Scotch snap," a short-long rhythmic pattern (), comes from the Lowland country.

The "Scotch turn," a pattern that moves up-down, or down-up, is also a distinctive feature of Scottish melody.

The bagpipe adds unique color to Scottish music. The wailing drone on an open fifth is its common sound. You can add a drone as an accompaniment to "Comin' Thro' the Rye." On the autoharp, hold down the G major and G minor chord buttons at the same time. Strum the strings near the center of the autoharp. Sing the melody beginning on D natural instead of D flat.

Migildi Magildi

Welsh Folk Song
Arranged by Kurt Miller
Words by Jack Dobbs

The people of Wales are well known for their song festivals and great choruses. From the earliest times Welshmen have sung in harmony, in contrast to the unison singing of many other ancient peoples.

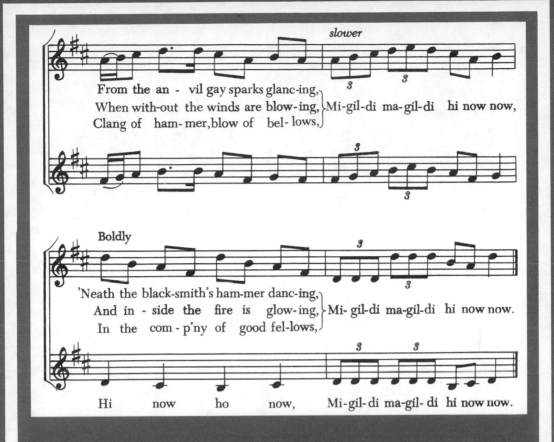

From the an - vil gay sparks glanc-ing,
When with-out the winds are blow-ing, } Mi-gil-di ma-gil-di hi now now,
Clang of ham-mer, blow of bel-lows,

Boldly

'Neath the black-smith's ham-mer danc-ing,
And in - side the fire is glow-ing, } Mi-gil-di ma-gil-di hi now now.
In the com - p'ny of good fel-lows,

Hi now ho now, Mi-gil-di ma-gil-di hi now now.

We know few Welsh songs because translation of the ancient Welsh language is difficult. In this work song, the ring of hammer and anvil may be sensed in the words and music of the song.

Begin by practicing the rhythm. Notice that sometimes the eighth notes are grouped in threes; sometimes they are grouped in twos. How will each group sound in relation to the beat? Practice this pattern to help you decide.

Greensleeves

Old English Folk Song

This song was popular during the reign of Queen Elizabeth I. Find out when that was. The title refers to the fact that the nobility could be identified by the colors they wore on their sleeves. Each "house" or family had a distinctive color.

1. A - las! my love,__ you do me wrong,__ To
2. Ah, Green - sleeves, now __ fare - well, a - dieu, __ To

cast me off __ dis - cour - teous - ly; For I have loved__ you,
God I pray __ to pros - per thee, For I am still __ thy

oh, so long,__ De - light - ing in __ your com - pa - ny.
sweet - heart true;__ Come once __ a - gain __ to meet __ me.

Refrain

Green - sleeves __ was all my joy, __ And oh, Green - sleeves __ was

my de - light, Green - sleeves,__ my heart of gold, __ And

all __ for La - dy Green - sleeves.

44

Listen to the recording. Notice the ancient instruments: the **viola da gamba, recorder,** and **lute.** Pluck this descant on a string instrument to suggest the sound of the lute.

Come, Follow Me

Round by
John Hilton

1. Come, fol - low, fol - low, fol - low, Fol - low, fol - low, fol - low me! Whith-er shall I fol - low, fol - low, fol - low, Whith - er shall I fol - low, fol - low thee? To the green-wood, to the green - wood, To the green - wood, green - wood tree.

45

Now Is the Month of Maying

Music by Thomas Morley

Listen to the recording of this famous madrigal by Thomas Morley. He was one of the most famous composers of the Golden Age. On the recording you first will hear the madrigal in a five-part instrumental arrangement. Then it is performed with voices singing the two parts that appear in your book, the other parts are played by instruments. Then voices sing the five-part madrigal as Morley wrote it.

la la la, Fa la la la la la la.

la la la, Fa la la la la la la.

(1.) Each with his bon - ny lass, A -
(2.) And to the bag - pipes' sound The

(1.) Each with his bon - ny lass, A -
(2.) And to the bag - pipes' sound The

danc - ing on the grass. ⎫
nymphs tread out the ground. ⎬ Fa la la la la,
                               ⎭

danc - ing on the grass. ⎫
nymphs tread out the ground. ⎬ Fa la la la la, Fa la
                               ⎭

Fa la la la la la la la la la la.

la la la. Fa la la la la la la.

Listen to this "rock" version of the song "Greensleeves" and compare it with the Elizabethean version found on page 44. The key has been changed to make it easier for you to accompany. What else has been changed?

A - las! my love, ____ you do me wrong, ____ To
I have loved ____ you oh, so long, ____ De -

cast me off ____ dis - cour - teous - ly; For

light - ing ____ in your com - pan - y.

Green - sleeves ____ was all my

BAH BAH BAH BAH BAH   *etc.*

joy ____ And oh, Green - sleeves ____ was

As you know, there are many performance styles under the general category of "rock," and different types of "rock" vary in sound. One of the features common to many of these styles is a slowly moving melody over a hard, driving rhythm. Listen for this in the version on your recording.

Here are some patterns you might use to build your own rock arrangement of "Greensleeves." They need not be loud, but must have a lot of energy.

Trumpet or **flute:** Play the harmony part on your instruments . . . Perform it crisply.

Autoharp: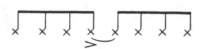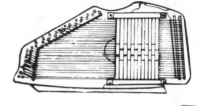

Tambourine: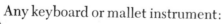

Cello: (use open strings)

For **Dm** chords   For **C** and **F** chords

For **A7** chords

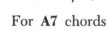  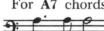

Any keyboard or mallet instrument:

Dm chords   **C** chords

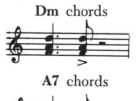 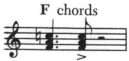

A7 chords

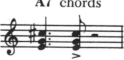

F chords

Golden Age of English Music

During the reign of Queen Elizabeth I, England was one of the most powerful countries in the world. Music played an important role in daily life, both at the Queen's court and in middle-class homes.

Many of the popular songs of the day were accompanied by the delicate plucking of **lute** strings. Listen to a composition for solo lute, "My Lady Hunsdon's Puffe," by John Dowland. Notice that the melody is varied each time it is repeated. The "Fantasia in G" is played on bowed string instruments called **viols**. Each viol plays its own melody. When more than one melody is played at one time, the result is called **polyphony,** which means "many sounds." Can you hear the polyphonic sections of "Lure, Falconers, Lure," a **madrigal** about hunting?

Dancing was a popular pastime among the English nobility. The two dance tunes you will hear, "Watkin's Ale" and "Munday's Joy," are performed by a group of recorders.

Old Abram Brown

Music by Benjamin Britten
Words Anonymous

Old A-bram Brown is dead and gone, You'll nev-er see him more.

He used to wear a long brown coat That but-toned down be-fore.

Tallis' Canon

Music by Thomas Tallis
Words by Thomas Ken

One person might learn to play this on an instrument such as the trumpet or clarinet. Then perform it with the class as a round. Voices may begin, and the instrument may enter as the second voice.

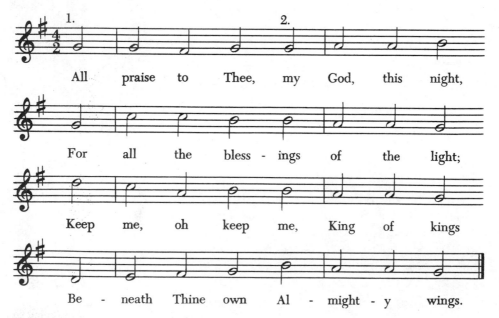

All praise to Thee, my God, this night,

For all the bless-ings of the light;

Keep me, oh keep me, King of kings

Be - neath Thine own Al - might - y wings.

IMPROVISATIONS FOR INSTRUMENTS

Idea I

Review this scale on your instrument.

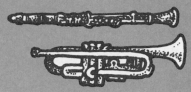

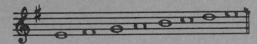

Then figure out the tune for "Old Abram Brown" by ear.

Perform in a group of three. Each performer plays the same melody, but in three different rhythms.

Player 1
(augmentation)

Player 2

Player 3
(diminution)

Idea II

Use these tones.

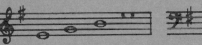

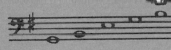

Play in $\frac{4}{4}$ meter, in any rhythm you find interesting.

Add your accompaniment to the melody in Idea I.

Idea III

Two persons take turns improvising a four-measure melody based on the "Old Abram Brown" tune. To improvise on a tune, take fragments of the melody and play them in different ways—higher or lower, backwards, in different rhythms.

Others may add an accompaniment using the ideas developed in Idea II.

A drummer can keep everyone together by playing a steady beat on a hand drum, or improvising a rhythm on a snare drum.

Blackbird

Words and Music by
John Lennon and
Paul McCartney

The melody of this lovely, contemporary song helps remind us that the English song tradition is still alive. John Lennon and Paul McCartney were part of the Beatles' group. Since the early 1960's when they first became popular, the Beatles have been a major influence on popular music. They broke up as a group in 1969 but have continued to contribute individually to current rock styles.

Study the song carefully. Discuss the melodic features and rhythmic changes which give the song its unique character. How many of the steps given on pages 11 and 22 can you complete as you learn the song?

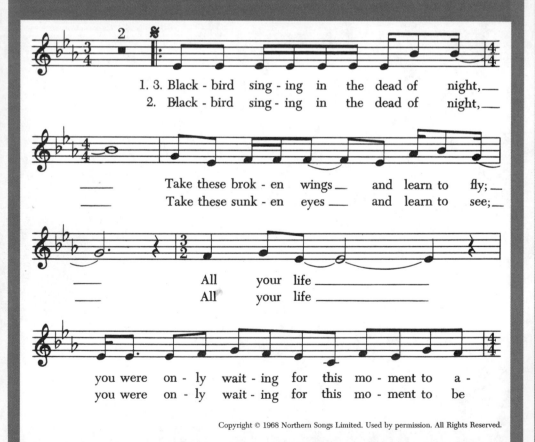

rise.　　　　　　　(2.) free.　　　(3.) rise.

Black - bird,___ fly, ___　Black - bird,___ fly ___

_____ in - to the light of a dark, black night.___

Young Person's Guide to the Orchestra

(Variations and Fugue on a Theme of Purcell)

by Benjamin Britten

Benjamin Britten used two themes in this composition. The first theme is by Henry Purcell, an English composer who lived three hundred years ago. For the second theme, Britten created a new melody.

The composition begins with Henry Purcell's theme played by full orchestra.

Listen carefully to the theme so you will recognize it later. Notice three important melodic characteristics: the upward leap in measure one, the turn up and down in measure two, and the sequence found in measures three, four, five, and six. After the theme is played by the orchestra, each family of the orchestra plays it in turn. The woodwinds begin.

Next it is played by the brass instruments.

Then the string instruments can be heard.

Finally the percussion instruments play the theme, followed by the full orchestra.

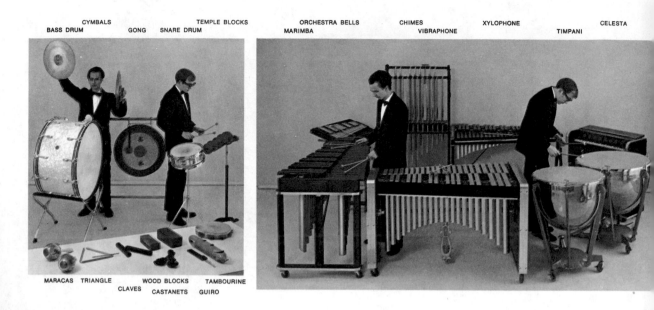

CYMBALS   TEMPLE BLOCKS   ORCHESTRA BELLS   CHIMES   XYLOPHONE   CELESTA
BASS DRUM   GONG   SNARE DRUM   MARIMBA   VIBRAPHONE   TIMPANI

MARACAS   TRIANGLE   WOOD BLOCKS   TAMBOURINE
CLAVES   CASTANETS   GUIRO

Now follow Britten's variations on the theme. Each features a particular instrument. The woodwinds begin, then the strings, followed by members of the brass family, and finally the percussion. Can you locate the picture of each solo instrument as it is heard?

As you listen to the different variations, notice ways Britten makes use of the three melodic characteristics of Purcell's theme.

When the variations are finished, Britten's own theme is played as a **fugue**.

The theme is played first by the piccolo, then by the other instruments in the same order as the variations. When you have heard this section, discuss the meaning of the term, "fugue."

How are the two themes used by the composer at the end of the composition?

Young Person's Guide to the Orchestra

by Benjamin Britten

First four measures from the full score:

A New Year Carol

Music by Benjamin Britten
Words Anonymous

Notice the different **marks of expression.** What does each one tell you to do as you sing?

1. Here we bring new wa-ter from the well ____ so clear,
2. Sing ____ reign of Fair Maid, with ____ gold up-on her toe,
3. Sing ____ reign of Fair Maid, with ____ gold up-on her chin,

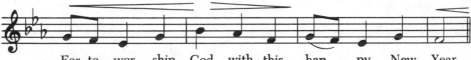

For to wor-ship God with this hap - py New Year.
O - pen you the West Door and turn the Old Year go.
O - pen you the East Door and let the New Year in.

Refrain

1., 2.

Sing le - vy dew, sing le - vy dew, the wa-ter and the wine;

The sev - en bright gold wires and the bu - gles that do shine.

3.

Sing le - vy dew, sing le - vy dew, the wa - ter and the

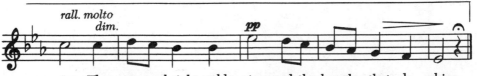

wine; The sev - en bright gold wires and the bu - gles that do shine.

Who Can Sail?

Swedish Folk Song
English Words Adapted by Rebecca Fenn

Girls (melody)

1. Who can sail when the winds don't blow?
2. I can sail when the winds don't blow;

Boys

1. Who can? Who can sail when the
2. I can. I can sail when the

Who can row with-out oars?
I can row with-out oars,

winds don't blow?
winds don't blow.

Who can leave an old trust - ed friend And
I can't leave an old trust - ed friend And

(Melody)

shed not a sin - gle tear?
shed not a sin - gle tear.

In Summer the Sunshine Is Brightest

Swedish Folk Song
Words Adapted

The countries of Scandinavia are lands of great contrast in climate, with long, dark winters and bright summers.

There is also great contrast in the songs of the Scandinavian people. Compare the mood of this Swedish song with the mood of "Who Can Sail?" page 59.

1. In sum - mer the sun - shine is bright - est;
2. In win - ter when cold winds are blow - ing,

The time when our hearts are the light - est.
We'll sit by the fire when it's snow - ing,

We walk through the wood and the mead - ow,
And dream of the bright sum - mer days When

And sing a joy - ful song, Hal - la, Hal - la!
we sang a joy - ful song, Hal - la, Hal - la!

Refrain

O come a - long and join our song;

The day is bright, our hearts are light.

When win - ter's done and fun's be - gun,

Our life is gay, you'll hear us say,

"In sum - mer the sun - shine is bright - est,

So sing a joy - ful song, Hal - la, Hal - la!"

I Came Home Late One Evening

Norwegian Folk Melody
Words Adapted

1. I came home late one eve-ning con-tent-ed and at rest,
2. I went to the sta-ble and bri-dled my grey steed;
3. I rode through the dark-ness and trav-eled five long miles.

But soon at my door came a knock-ing.
I knew he could run fast as light-ning.
The town was at rest sleep-ing sweet-ly.

A mes-sen-ger stood, and he said, "Go to your love,
The sad-dle was sil-ver, the reins were made of gold,
And when I ar-rived at the house of my love,

Ride quick-ly now to her dwell-ing."
And in the pale moon they shone bright-ly.
Her broth-er was wait-ing to meet me.

O my love, my on-ly love, my dear one.

4. We quickly went inside and I asked about my love.
   He burst out in sorrow a-crying.
   So sad were his words, that I thought my heart would break
   To hear that my loved one was dying.
   O my love, my only love, my dear one.

5. I walked for a while through the meadows and the hills,
   And nearby the church bells were tolling.
   My heart was so sad, that I could not bear to stay;
   I knew far away I'd be going.
   O my love, my only love, my dear one.

Music by a Norwegian Composer: Edvard Grieg

for voice:

Grieg is the most famous of the Norwegian composers. His music is often based on Norwegian folk melodies and rhythms. Music of this type is called **nationalistic** music.

"Solveig's Song" was written for the play, *Peer Gynt*. Peer Gynt was a young man who spent his life searching for adventure. Solveig was the girl who loved him and waited for him.

Listen to "Solveig's Song." Notice that part of Grieg's melody is exactly like that of "I Came Home Late One Evening." In what other ways are the two songs similar?

for piano:

This piano composition by Grieg also is based on a folk tune. The melody was originally played on a fiddle and was used as an accompaniment for a folk dance called the "Halling." Listen to the fiddle tune and imagine the dance. It is a vigorous reel with many high kicks. Good dancers sometimes turn somersaults in time to the music.

When you have enjoyed the fiddle tune, listen to Grieg's piano music. What is its design? When do you hear the fiddle tune? When do you hear musical ideas that are Grieg's own?

Totur

Danish Folk Dance

"Totur" means "two around," and the dance of this name is a couple dance done in a circle. It is a "mixer" and is a popular dance in the United States as well as in Denmark. The dance is based on the "two-step," which is done in the pattern step-together-step.

With partners in ballroom position, practice the two-step in preparation for learning "Totur." Listen to the record to get acquainted with the rhythm; then practice the two-step with the music.

The dance is composed of an introduction and two parts. During the introduction, partners walk in the circle 16 steps to the left, 16 steps to the right.

In part one of the dance, partners move to the center of the circle in the pattern: step-together-step, walk, walk. Return to your place with the same steps. Then do four two-steps, turning as you move around the ring.

Repeat all of part one, and finish facing your partner.

In part two of the dance, do a grand right and left for 16 measures.

Take a new partner.

Repeat part one of the dance.

Viking Picture Stone

Icelandic Prayer

Icelandic Folk Song

(Melody in lower part)

1. O great God of the earth,
2. O great mak - er of life,

Hear now my prayer ris - ing up - ward,
Give now my spir - it Thy beau - ty,

Wak - en my soul to Thy good!
Fill all my days with Thy work!

Wak - en my soul to Thy good!
Fill all my days with Thy work!

The Norwegian Vikings settled Iceland in the ninth century. The ancient language and music which they brought with them have survived since that time. The music is much like the church music of the ninth century, particularly the use of the interval of the fifth between the voice parts. Singing in parallel fifths was the earliest kind of harmony.

Music of Western Europe

Although the countries of Western Europe border each other very closely, each has developed a distinctive national character. Each has its own language, social customs, and folk music, all of which reflect the special character of each region. These countries also have a long heritage of composed music. Most of the musical forms we know were developed by European composers.

This rich tradition is due in part to the early support of the church, which employed musicians for religious services. A music master, who was also a composer, was hired to direct the church choir. Toward the end of the middle ages, the European nobility began to play a more important role in the support of musical life. Each court had a staff of musicians who performed for the nobleman and his friends. Again, the director was usually a composer and was expected to write new music for many different occasions.

As trade and commerce developed in Europe, the middle class had more time and money to enjoy music and the arts. Large halls and opera houses were built for public concerts. Even today, visitors to Europe are enjoying concerts in these same halls. In the churches and cathedrals of Germany, France, and Italy, many of the organs built centuries ago are still being used for services. And, of course, European composers of today continue to experiment with new sounds and styles of performance.

Ma bella bimba

Italian Folk Song
Arranged by Kurt Miller
Words Adapted

Ma co-me bal - li, bel-la bim - ba, bel - la
bim - ba, bel-la bim - ba, Ma co-me bal - li, bel - la
bim - ba, bel - la bim - ba, bal - li ben!

Ma co - me bel -
la bim-ba, Ma co - me
bel - la ben!

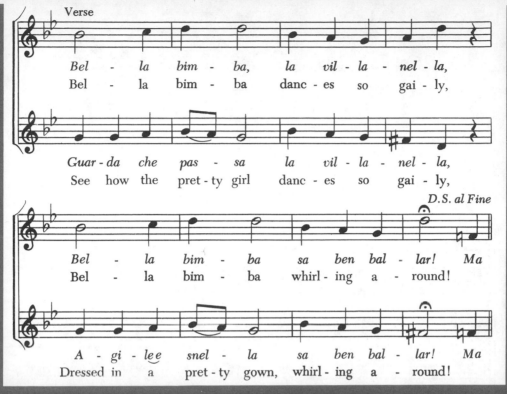

Verse

Bel - la bim - ba, la vil - la - nel - la,
Bel - la bim - ba danc - es so gai - ly,

Guar - da che pas - sa la vil - la - nel - la,
See how the pret - ty girl danc - es so gai - ly,

D.S. al Fine

Bel - la bim - ba sa ben bal - lar! Ma
Bel - la bim - ba whirl - ing a - round!

A - gi - le e snel - la sa ben bal - lar! Ma
Dressed in a pret - ty gown, whirl - ing a - round!

Follow the instructions on page 22 and learn the melody. Your answers for the verse and for the refrain may be different. When you know the melody, some of you may learn the harmony part.

Italian folk songs are of many types. There are boat songs of Venice, street songs of Naples, and romantic songs and dances of Sicily. Italian folk songs are often lively and bright. Many of the melodies change from minor to major at the refrain. They often are quite ornamented and cover a wide range. The rhythms are lightly accented and dance-like. A sprightly refrain may follow a quiet verse. Favorite Italian folk instruments are the guitar, mandolin, and concertina. These are used to accompany songs and dances.

Study "Ma bella bimba." Which of the features named above can you find in this song? Add an autoharp accompaniment to suggest the sound of the Italian string instruments.

Italy is a land of music and art. The country is noted for singers, opera, cathedrals, paintings, and almost every type of fine art one can name. The country is represented by five artists and their works in the art section of your book.

The Silver Moon Is Shining

Italian Folk Song

Macaroni

(I Maccheroni)

Neapolitan Folk Song
English Words Adapted

Tempo of Tarantella

Boys

1. I'm so poor, hear what I'm say - in,' I've no
2. I would like to be a sol - dier In the
3. My lieu - ten - ant, oh, so ar - dent, Changed his

Girls

bed nor place to stay in. You'd best sell your shirt for
ar - my, like I told 'ya. Push the can - non, pull the
place with his own ser - geant. Sold his rank to get your

mon - ey, 'Fat - ten you up with mac - a - ro - ni.
po - ny, Still buy a dish of mac - a - ro - ni.
mon - ey; Now he will eat your mac - a - ro - ni.

Together

Ven - de - rei i miei cal - zo - ni, Per un sol

piat - to di mac - che - ro - ni.

Zim, Zim

Spanish Canon

Learn this round by following the instructions on pages 11 and 22. Then listen to the recording to learn the Spanish words. The song imitates the sounds of different instruments.

Zim, zim, zim ha - ce el vio - lín, ___ drin, drin, drin el gui - ta - rrín, ___ zum, zum, zum el con - tra - ba - jo, ta, ta, ta el cuer - no a - llá.

Noche de feria

Flamenco Dance Melody
from Seville

Listen to the Spanish guitarist play in **flamenco** style. Flamenco is a style of gypsy dance and dance music. It has been used in compositions for the guitar by many composers.

As you listen, notice how the performer alternates between plucking the melody on a single string and strumming the chords in exciting rhythms. It is these rhythmic passages which are usually associated with the flamenco style.

La Tarara

Spanish Folk Song

Refrain

La Ta - ra - ra, sí, la Ta - ra - ra, no,

Fine

la Ta - ra - ra, ni - ña, que la he vis - to yo.

Verse

1. Lle - va mi Ta - ra - ra un ves - ti - do ver - de,
2. Lu - ce mi Ta - ra - ra sus co - las de se - da

D.C. al Fine

lle - no de vo - lan - tes y de cas - ca - be - les.
en - tre las re - ta - mas y la hier - ba - bue - na.

Listen to the recording. Notice the accompaniment played by tambourine, castanets, and small drum. Here is a rhythm pattern played by the castanets.

Can you write the patterns played by the other instruments? Three people may play them as the class sings.

Le Cid Ballet Suite

Castillane, Andalouse,
Aragonaise, Aubade

by Jules Massenet

The dances of this suite are examples of Spanish influence in music. Massenet and many other French composers were fascinated by the music they heard and the folk dances they saw when they visited Spain. It is easy for us to imagine the original street dances, songs, and instruments which inspired Massenet to write this music for orchestra.

Castillane

"Castillane," an animated dance in $\frac{6}{8}$ rhythm, takes its name from the Spanish province of Castile. It is a rondo—the rhythm and melody of the first theme return many times and alternate with less important themes.

A special feature is the rhythm which is heard through most of the composition.

Andalouse

"Andalouse" takes its name from the southern province of Andalusia and shows the Moorish influence in Spanish music. The melodies move slowly over the habanera rhythm.

Both themes are in the key of A minor, and the design is one with which you are familiar.

Aragonaise

"Aragonaise" imitates sounds the composer heard in the province of Aragon. Listen to the recording, and discuss how he incorporated the folk sounds. Why is the music exciting even though it includes only one important melody?

Aubade

"Aubade" means "morning serenade." Which sounds of the orchestra give the music its charm?

Choose one of the dances from *Le Cid* and create your own Spanish dance. Use Spanish dance ideas you have seen, and experiment until you find a foot pattern and dance movement for each melody. Decide on a formation, combine your dance ideas, and dance as you listen to the music. Accompany your dance with instruments.

My Homeland

German Folk Melody
Arranged by Johannes Brahms
English Words by
Franz Wilhelm

Learn this song by singing the numbers. Then add your own accompaniment by following the suggestions on page 27. Play your accompaniment on bells or on the piano.

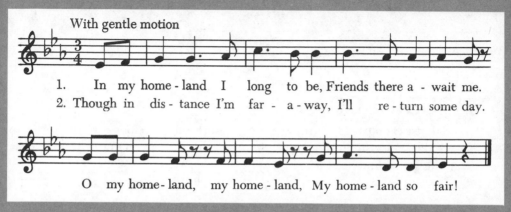

This folk melody was arranged by Johannes Brahms, an important German composer. Listen to the recording. Compare your accompaniment with that of Brahms. Did you use the same chords? In Brahm's accompaniment notice how the broken chords and the strong bass line, with a melody of its own, add interest to the simple melody.

Songs which express feelings about homeland and about the activities of daily life have long been a part of German folk-song literature. Many of the songs are solid and vigorous; others are sentimental. Most are based on the major scale.

Part singing is common among the Germans. They usually improvise harmonizing parts in thirds and sixths. Many German folk songs have strongly accented dance-like rhythms. Many of their dances move in threes. The *Ländler*, a traditional dance, is the ancestor of the modern waltz.

Du, du liegst mir im Herzen

German Folk Song
Arranged by Mary Val Marsh

In waltz rhythm

Du, du liegst mir im Her - zen,

Du, du liegst mir im Sinn,

Du, du machst mir viel Schmer - zen,

Weisst nicht, wie gut ich dir bin; _____

Tra la la la la la la Tra la la la la

(Melody)

Ja, ja, ja, ja,

la _____ la la la. _____

Weisst nicht, wie gut ich dir bin. _____

Evening Prayer

by Engelbert Humperdinck

Humperdinck, like Brahms, often turned to folk music for his musical ideas. The prayer is taken from the opera *Hansel and Gretel* which is based on a folktale and contains many folk melodies.

This song is a good example of two types of harmony. Notice that the parts move together during the first phrase. This type of harmony is called **homophonic**. **Homo** means "one"; **phonic** means "sound." Therefore, **homophonic** means "tones sounding together as one." In the last part of the song the voices move independently, each with its own important melody. Do you remember the name of this type of music? Refer to page 49 if you do not remember.

When at night I go to sleep, Four-teen an-gels watch do_ keep,

When at night I go to sleep,_ Four-teen an-gels watch do_ keep,

Two my head are guard-ing, Two my feet are guid-ing,

Two my head are guard-ing, Two my feet are guid-ing,

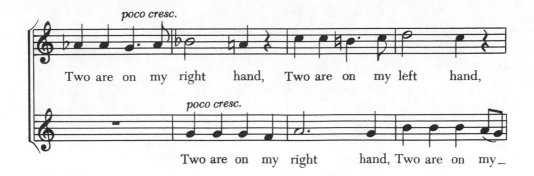

poco cresc.

Two are on my right hand, Two are on my left hand,

poco cresc.

Two are on my right hand, Two are on my_

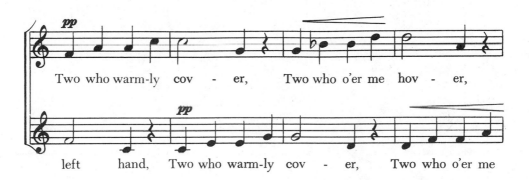

pp

Two who warm-ly cov - er, Two who o'er me hov - er,

pp

left hand, Two who warm-ly cov - er, Two who o'er me

Two to whom 'tis giv - en To guide my steps to

hov - er, Two who guide my steps to

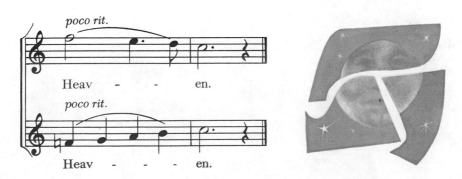

poco rit.

Heav - - en.

poco rit.

Heav - - en.

81

Egmont Overture

by Ludwig van Beethoven

Of the many musical messages of freedom, none is more stirring than this overture. It is named for Count Egmont who, before the year 1600, inspired the Dutch to unite against their Spanish conquerors. Although he was imprisoned and eventually executed, his leadership continued to inspire the people, and the Dutch were eventually victorious.

Listen to Beethoven's overture, and enjoy the powerful music. It begins with a great chord in which all of the instruments unite as did the people of the Netherlands. The music which follows expresses the woe of the people, their restlessness, the confidence they gained, the uprising, and finally, the proclamation of victory.

The proclamation is heard in the coda. Beethoven called it his "Little Symphony of Victory." The coda begins with a restless murmuring of kettledrums and strings and then the call to arms.

The coda moves on with the theme of battle

and closes with the triumphant theme of victory.

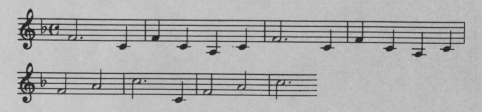

This is a composition you can enjoy hearing many times because you will always discover something new. Each time you listen, try to hear more and more musical details.

1. The strong chords of the opening section.

2. A melody pattern played first by violins, repeated many times in sequence.

3. Egmont's theme, a descending melody played first by cellos and later by the violins.

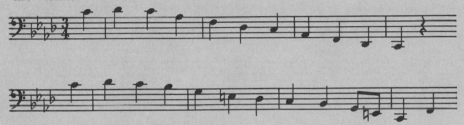

4. A dialogue between strings and woodwinds.

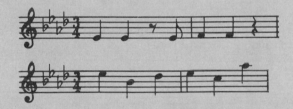

5. A section including scale passages, followed by repeated melody patterns in the woodwinds.

6. The return of Egmont's theme and the woodwind-string dialogue.

7. A new dialogue between brass and strings.

8. The coda.

Beethoven is considered by many to be the greatest of all composers. He wrote hundreds of works for almost every instrument known in his time. Yet it is something more that seems important to the lovers of Beethoven's music. It is the composer's ability to reach the hearts and minds of those who perform his music and those who listen to it. The composition is also a fine example of the way in which the man and his ideals are expressed in his music.

The Herdsman

German-Swiss Folk Song
Arranged by Kurt Miller

1. Hol - la, Hol - li, sings all day long;_
2. Hol - la, Hol - li, climb moun-tains tall;_

(Melody)

1. The_ herds - man_ is _ mer - ry, he_ sings all day long,
2. The_ cows keep_ Hans_ bus - y as they climb moun-tains tall,

Hol - la, Hol - li, sings this gay song.
Hol - la, Hol - li, ech - o - ing call.

And_ while he_ is _ tend - ing, he_ sings this gay song.
And at eve - ning_ Hans_ waits for Hei- di's ech - o - ing call.

Refrain
(Melody)

Hol - li - a, Hol - li - a, li - a - lo; Hol -

Hol - li - a, la - lo;

li - a, Hol - li - a, li - a lay. lay.

Hol - li - a, la - lay. lay.

Blacksmith's Dance

German Folk Dance

Listen to this rollicking dance in waltz rhythm. The music is played by a German band. Which instruments do you hear? The style is typical of the music of German folk dances.

The music begins with a four-measure introduction. Then the melody is played. Clap the accents of the waltz rhythm. How many accents do you clap as you hear the melody once? How many times is the melody repeated? How do the repetitions sound different?

There are four patterns to learn in the dance—the clap patterns, circles, stars, and the do-si-do. The dance closes with a "fireworks" ending. Practice each pattern. Dance the entire dance in vigorous style.

Allelujah

French Canon

You may sing this round in as many as eight parts! Your voices in harmony will suggest the sounds of the bells in the French cathedrals.

The folk music of France, like the music of other countries you have studied, is widely varied. There are religious songs, such as the simple round on this page. There are also many work songs. Other songs recall important historical events.

Some of the folk melodies are based on ancient scales known as **modes**. Other songs are pentatonic. Folk melodies often move by scale steps and have little ornamentation. The range of the work song is usually narrow, while other types of songs have a wider range.

The words are important in French songs, and the phrases may vary in length to suit the text. The rhythm often follows the natural word stress, which results in irregular measures. In some songs the rhythms are taken from dances.

Plowing Song

French Folk Song
Words Translated

Follow instructions on page 11 and learn the rhythm. Chant the words lightly until the irregular rhythms move smoothly.

1. "O plow, farm-er, plow! My fence is sure to break." "O did you say, my mas-ter, I must not work so late?"— O - lay.

2. "O no, farm-er, no! I said that you must plow." "O did you say, my mas-ter, I'd bet-ter feed the cow?"— O - lay.

Refrain

O - lay, O - lay, O - lay, O - lay, ___ O - lay, O - lay, ___ O - lay. ___

Which characteristics of French folk music can you find in this song?

The **musette**, an instrument similar to the bagpipe, often is heard in French folk music. Imitate its sound by playing F and C on the piano or on a string instrument. Play the chord at the beginning of each measure.

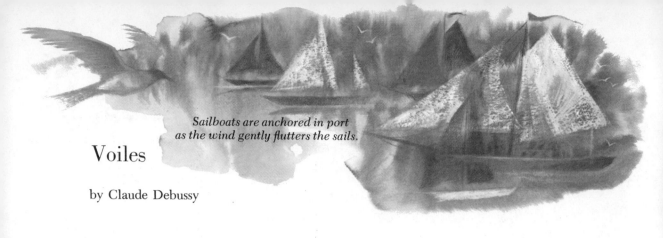

Sailboats are anchored in port as the wind gently flutters the sails.

Voiles

by Claude Debussy

The composer Debussy added the words above to the score of his piano piece "Voiles," or "Sails." This music captures in sound the play of light on the water and the shimmering movement of the sails.

Debussy found that the major and minor scales and traditional musical forms did not allow him to express his ideas. He searched for new techniques of writing music and developed a new style of his own.

The melody of "Voiles" is based on a **whole-tone scale.** Look at the opening melody given below. (The pitches are written an octave lower than you hear them on the recording.) Play the melody in the bells. How does the whole-tone scale differ from major and minor scales?

The harmony also comes from the whole-tone scale. Here are some of the chords Debussy uses. How are they different from chords that you are accustomed to hearing?

Debussy's new style, **impressionism,** helped other composers realize that music need not always follow the old rules. It encouraged them to search for new ways to organize musical sound. Composers are still inventing new ways of writing music, some of them based on Debussy's ideas.

Listen again to a portion of "Farandole" on page 30. Compare the style of that composition with "Voiles." Consider rhythm, pitch, texture, tone color, design, and dynamics.

Compose Impressionistic Music

Work in groups of four. Compose a musical impression. Use **augmented chords** similar to those used in "Voiles."

Players 1, 2, 3:
Play an **accompaniment.**
Use the chords shown in the graph.

Which meter will you use?
Play a chord once per measure.

In what order will you play the chords?

Play your part on bells, piano, or a band or orchestral instrument.

Player 4
Improvise a **melody** over the accompaniment.
Use only those tones shown on the chart.

Give your melody a rhythm which moves more frequently than the accompaniment.

Choose a descriptive title for your musical impression.

Try building another musical impression using **diminished chords.**

Would the same descriptive title be appropriate for this composition?

Compare the augmented and diminished chords you played with major and minor chords. How do they differ in sound? What reasons can you find for the differences?

Can you build augmented, diminished, major, and minor chords starting on other pitches?

Music of Eastern Europe and the Soviet Union

In early times, the countries of Eastern Europe and the Balkan peninsula were often invaded by such groups as the Mongols, the Turks, and the Romans. Each invading nation brought the influences of its language, customs, and music. As a result, the folk music of Eastern Europe is a fascinating blend of exotic sounds.

Composers of this region have long been intrigued by their own folk traditions. You can find many old folk tunes and dance forms in the music of such composers as Bartók and Smetana.

As you study the music of Eastern Europe, compare it with the Western European music that you know. Can you think of some reasons for the similarities and differences?

Glockenjodler

Austrian Folk Song
Arranged by Egon Kraus

Variations On A Fishy Theme

Piano Quintet in A ("The Trout")

Fourth Movement

by Franz Schubert

You have heard compositions in **theme and variation** form.
Have you ever composed your own?

What are some ways a theme can be varied? Add to this list.

Vary a

melody by. . . . . adding extra tones to "**ornament**" the melody.

. . . changing from major to minor.

harmony by. . . . . adding **countermelodies** above the theme.

rhythm by. . . . . changing the **even** rhythm of a melody to an **uneven** rhythm.

timbre by . . . . giving the melody to various instruments.

musical controls by . . . . playing louder—softer.

. . . playing *staccato—legato*.

Now listen to a set of variations on a theme. The theme is the melody of a song called "The Trout." As you listen, write down the techniques from your list which the composer used in his variations. There are six variations, so you will need to have six separate lists.

93

The Peddler

Ukrainian Folk Song
Words by Margaret Lowrey

The minor quality and strongly accented rhythm of this song are typical of music from Russia. As you listen to the recording, notice that the accompaniment suggests the sound of the **balalaika**, a popular Russian string instrument.

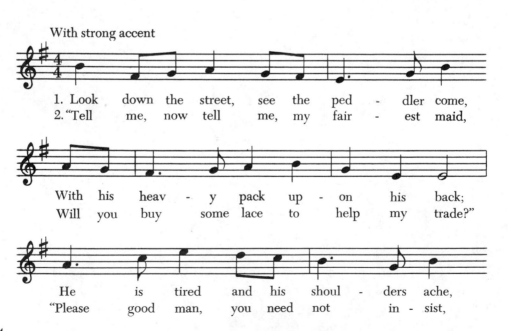

With strong accent

1. Look down the street, see the ped - dler come,
2. "Tell me, now tell me, my fair - est maid,

With his heav - y pack up - on his back;
Will you buy some lace to help my trade?"

He is tired and his shoul - ders ache,
"Please good man, you need not in - sist,

But he must move on for mon - ey's sake.
For such love - ly lace I can't re - sist."

Refrain

Hai - da, hai - da, hai - da, hai - da, ___

Hai - da, hai - da, hai - da, da.

Boys, sing this harmonizing part while the girls sing the melody. To read the notes of your part, you must be able to read the **bass clef.**

Here is the **grand staff** which is made up of the **bass clef** and the **treble clef.** In singing, men usually read the low pitches as shown on the bass clef. Women read the higher pitches as shown on the treble clef.

Minka

Russian Folk Song
English Words by W. S. Haynie

Here is a two-part song for you to sing. In what clef is the lower part written? Who should sing it? Can you sing the notes with letter names? Then sing with "loo," and finally sing the words. Sing the two parts together.

1. Min - ka, Min - ka, when I leave thee, How my sad heart
2. When I hear sweet mu - sic play - ing, Ev - ery note to

1. Min - ka, Min - ka, when I
2. When I hear sweet mu - sic

al - ways grieves me. When I'm gone I long to be with
me is say - ing, Min - ka, Min - ka, fair - est maid - en,

leave thee, How my sad heart
play - ing, Ev - ery note to

Min - ka, Min - ka mine. When I
Min - ka, Min - ka mine. When the
(Melody)

al - ways grieves _ me. When I see the
me is say - ing: When the win - ter

96

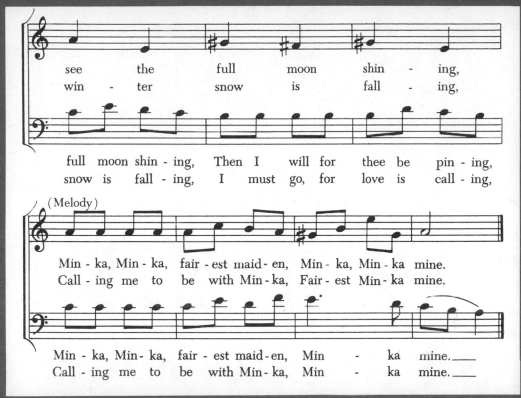

see the full moon shin - ing,
win - ter snow is fall - ing,

full moon shin - ing, Then I will for thee be pin - ing,
snow is fall - ing, I must go, for love is call - ing,

(Melody)

Min - ka, Min - ka, fair - est maid - en, Min - ka, Min - ka mine.
Call - ing me to be with Min - ka, Fair - est Min - ka mine.

Min - ka, Min - ka, fair - est maid - en, Min - ka mine.____
Call - ing me to be with Min - ka, Min - ka mine.____

Start on A, and arrange the pitches in the first three measures from low to high. Notice the "gap" between the sixth and seventh tones. Gapped scales such as this are often found in songs from Russia and Eastern Europe. What scale do you know that sounds almost the same?

Song of the Volga Boatmen

Russian Folk Song

Russian musicians have long been known for their expressive singing. Listen to this performance of a famous Russian folk song, "Song of the Volga Boatmen." Notice the singer's wide range and rich, deep tone quality. Listen to the way he adds to the expressive nature of the song by using various dynamics.

The haunting melody and rhythmic drive of this song are typical of Russian musical style. The balalaika orchestra which accompanies the singer is also representative. The balalaika is a string instrument with a triangular body and a long, fretted neck. It usually has three strings which are strummed with a **plectrum**. Balalaikas are made in six sizes.

Symphony No. 5, Opus 47

Movement Two (Allegretto)

by Dmitri Shostakovich

How good are your ears and eyes? can you match the melodies you see with what you hear?

Determine the correct order as you listen.

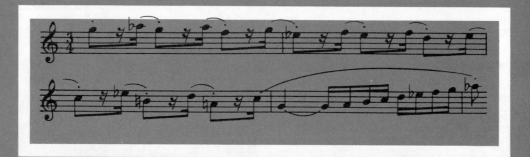

Far in the Mountains

Finnish Folk Song
Words Adapted

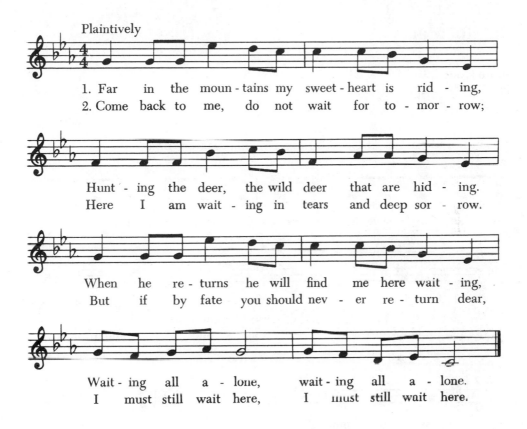

1. Far in the moun-tains my sweet-heart is rid-ing,
2. Come back to me, do not wait for to-mor-row;

Hunt-ing the deer, the wild deer that are hid-ing.
Here I am wait-ing in tears and deep sor-row.

When he re-turns he will find me here wait-ing,
But if by fate you should nev-er re-turn dear,

Wait-ing all a-lone, wait-ing all a-lone.
I must still wait here, I must still wait here.

Play this descant on an instrument such as the flute, oboe, or violin. On the recording the descant is played by the French horn an octave lower than written here. Listen for the distinctive sound of this instrument which is accompanied by the harp.

Friend, Since You Want to Marry

Greek Folk Song
English Words Adapted

Many songs and dances of Greece have irregular meter. Practice this rhythm.

Greek dan - ces move in sev - ens, Greek dan - ces move in sev - ens.

1. Friend, since you want to mar - ry, To take a wife, Come
2. Oh, don't take a fair wom - an, A sack of flour, Of
3. And don't take a dark wom - an, A dark plump grape, A

ask _____ me. 1. Friend, ask _____ me. And I'll
white ____ flour. 2. Oh, white ____ flour, For a
plump ___ grape. 3. And plump ___ grape, For a

tell you which __ girl __ will ____ do, And the
sack of flour ___ is ___ dust - y, And too
grape be - comes __ a ___ rai - sin, Yes, an

ones that are not __ good for you. And I'll good for you.
mess - y, you will __ a - gree. For a a - gree.
old wrin - kled dried __ rai - sin. For a rai - sin.

Softly Calls the Cuckoo

Bulgarian Folk Song
English Words by William Stracke

Divide into two groups. Some may sing this chant while others sing the melody.

Cuck - oo, __ cuck - oo! Cuck - oo, __ cuck - oo!

Moderately

1. Soft - ly calls the cuck - oo From the bud - ding beech tree,
2. Brave - ly calls the cuck - oo To the scat - tered he - roes:
3. Sad - ly calls the cuck - oo In the moun - tain fast - ness,

Ech - o - ing the prom - ise That each new spring brings us,
"Rise a - gain and drive out Strang - ers from our low - lands.
Mourn - ing for the fall - en; Ask - ing of the liv - ing:

Shed - ding bonds of win - ter.
Hail our an - cient glo - ries."
"What be - came of free - dom?"

IRREGULAR METER

Stamp, clap, and speak the following chant.

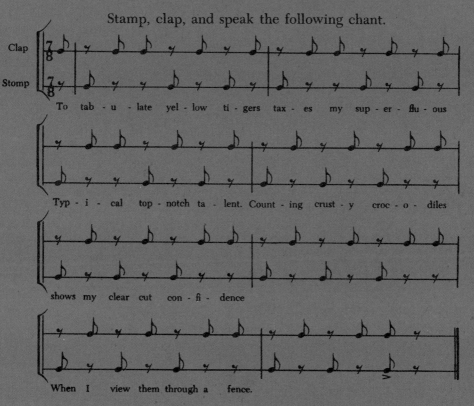

Make up your own nonsense chants. Use irregular meters.
Make a list of two, three, four, and five-syllable words such as:
tintinnabular   tigeroo   fantabulous   zero   zeppelin   zig-zag   zany
Use nonsense words, odd-sounding words, unusual words.
Combine them in a chant in

$\frac{5}{4}$ (Group the five beats 3 + 2
or 2 + 3)

$\frac{7}{8}$ (Group the seven beats 3 + 2 + 2
or 2 + 2 + 3)

Maintain a steady beat by stamping and clapping.

Misirlú, Greek Folk Dance

Listen to this traditional Greek music. When you are familiar with its
rhythm and melody, learn the dance.

102

The Moldau

by Bedřich Smetana

Listen to "The Moldau" by Smetana. The Moldau is the chief river in Czechoslovakia, the composer's homeland. This **tone poem** is an example of **nationalism** in music. When you know the composition, use it as an example and define the two musical terms.

Smetana wrote this description as a preface to his music.

> Two springs start their courses in a shady Bohemian forest: one is warm and sparkling, the other cool and tranquil. Their clear waters that run so gayly over stone and pebble unite and sparkle in the morning sun. The rapid forest brook, rushing on, becomes the River Moldau. As it takes its course through the fields and valleys of Bohemia, it grows into a mighty river. The river flows through dense forests from where the joyous clanging sound of the hunter's horn seems to approach the listener.

> It makes its way through meadows and farms. A rustic wedding is being joyfully celebrated with music and song and dance. The water nymphs are seen by moonlight in the river's glittering waters. Reflected towers and castles are reminders of the past glory of chivalry and martial fame. At St. John's Rapids the stream winds its way through the foamy rapids of the cataract and through the deep and narrow rocky cleft into the broad river bed. It rolls majestically on to Prague, welcomed on its way by the old castle Vysehrad, and disappears in the distance from the composer's vision.

What kind of music do you expect to hear? How will it begin? How will it continue? As you listen, try to associate what you hear with the scenes Smetana describes. What musical devices does he use to help you imagine the river, the scenes, and the activities along the bank?

Riding Song

Czechoslovakian Folk Song
Words by Martha C. Ramsey

This spirited, rhythmic melody is typical of the music of Czechoslovakia. The triple meter, the long tone at the end of the phrase, the stepwise melody, and the insertion of the exclamation between the verse and refrain are characteristic of Czech music.

With spirit

1. Came a - rid - ing on a day,
2. Oft he asked in man - ner bold, } Zum - ta - dy - ja - dy - ja;
3. Now my heart I'd give to you,

A suit - or jaun - ty, bold and gay,
How could I my heart with - hold? } Zum - ta - dy - ja - dy - ja, *Hey!*
Could I be sure your own were true,

Refrain

Zum - ta - dy - ja - dy - ja, zum - ta - dy - ja - da,

La la la la la la la la

zum - ta - dy - ja - dy - ja, zum - ta - dy - ja - da; Zum - ta - dy - ja - dy - ja,

la la la la la la la la La la la

zum - ta - dy - ja - da,   zum - ta - dy - ja - dy - ja.

la   la la la la la   la la la   la la.

Evening Air

Hungarian Folk Song
English Words by
Betty Askwith

1.   2.   3.   4.

Sweet the eve - ning air of May,   Soft my cheek ca - ress - ing;

Fine

Sweet the un - seen li - lac spray With its scent - ed bless - ing.

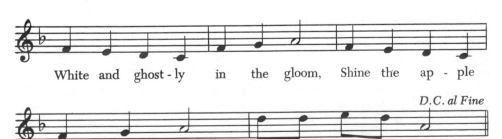

White and ghost - ly   in   the   gloom,   Shine the   ap - ple

D.C. al Fine

trees   in   bloom,   ap - ple   trees   in   bloom.

Farewell, Beloved Homeland

Music by Béla Bartók
Words Adapted

Bartók is a modern Hungarian composer. He became interested in Hungarian folk music early in the twentieth century and collected and arranged many long-forgotten songs. Music composed by Bartók also shows his interest in the music of his homeland. The close harmonies, exotic scales, unusual intervals, and changing rhythms of the folk song can be heard in many of his compositions.

O fare-well, be-lov-ed home-land. Sad I leave my Mag-yar

home-land. Oft in my dreams,__ I see your hills,__

Mem-'ries of their beau-ty haunt me. Oft in my dreams,__

I see your hills,__ Mem-'ries of their beau-ty haunt me.

"Elindultan Szep Hazambul" by Béla Bartók, copyright by Zenemukiado Vallalat.
Reprinted by permission of Boosey and Hawkes, Inc., sole agents for Kultura.

SYNTHETICS

Do you know the meaning of the word **synthetic**?
Can you decide what a **synthetic scale** would be?

You have played major scales   `1` `2` `3` `4` `5` `6` `7` `8` **(1)**

minor scales   `1` `2` `3` `4` `5` `6` `7` `8` **(1)**

whole-tone scales   `1` `2` `3` `4` `5` `6` `1`

Plan a **synthetic scale** of six tones.
Plan a sequence of **whole** and **half** steps that is different from other scales
you know.

Interval size   `1` `?` `?` ` ` ` ` ` ` ` ` ` ` ` ` ` `

Make a graph such as the one above and plot your intervals on it.
Start on C and play your new scale. Which pitches did you use?
Use your new scale to make up a melody for a familiar rhyme such as:

> Jack be nimble, Jack be quick.
> Jack jump over the candlestick.

Bartók sometimes used synthetic scales in his music.
Here is part of a composition for two violins. Play it on violins or bells.
Can you figure out the synthetic scale he made up for this duet?

Symphony No. 40 in G minor

First and Third Movements

by Wolfgang Amadeus Mozart

The illustrations below suggest the design of two movements of one of Mozart's symphonies. Compare the two designs. Which parts are repeated? Where are new ideas introduced?

Listen to the **minuet** and follow its design. How many large sections does the minuet have? How are the themes arranged within the sections?

THIRD MOVEMENT

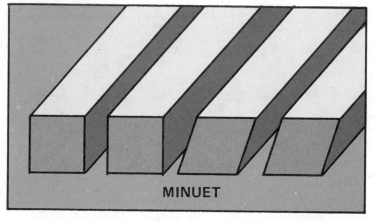

MINUET

TRIO

FIRST MOVEMENT

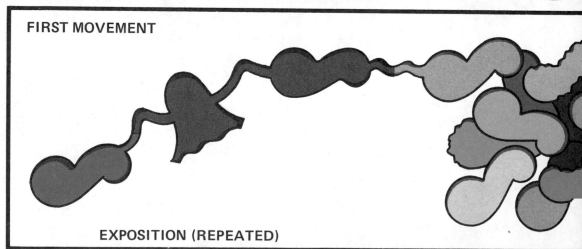

EXPOSITION (REPEATED)

Now listen to the **first movement.** In what ways does the design differ from that of the third movement?

The minuet form is sometimes described as **A B A.** The first-movement form is sometimes described as **Exposition—Development—Recapitulation.** Why are the two movements described differently?

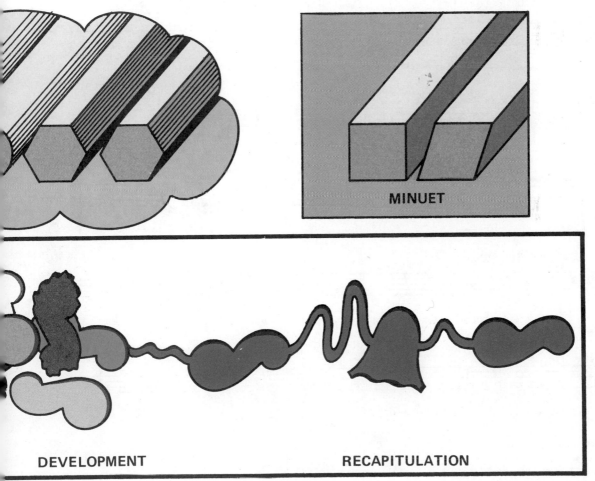

MINUET

DEVELOPMENT   RECAPITULATION

Many American folk melodies lend themselves to performance in contemporary styles. Listen to a folk-rock version of "Bound for the Promised Land."

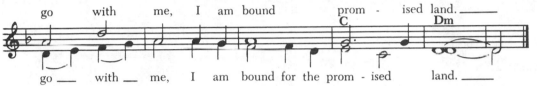

go   with   me,   I   am   bound   prom - ised land. _____

go __ with __ me,   I   am   bound for the prom - ised   land. _____

What characteristics of rock music do you hear?   country music?

Choose several of these patterns and combine them for your own folk-rock arrangement.

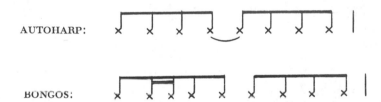

AUTOHARP:

BONGOS:

CELLO:

for **Dm** and **B♭** chords.   for **C** chords   for **Am** chords

Listen to a "Gospel-revival" version of the same song. In what ways have melody and rhythm been changed?

The Musician at Work... in a Recording Studio

Have you ever wondered how a record is made? Recording just one song requires the time and effort of more people than you might have guessed.

The **Studio Engineer** operates all of the recording equipment. He sets up the tapes, adjusts levels of sound, and offers help and suggestions to the performers when they need special sound effects.

The **Music Director** or **Producer** is in charge of coordinating the recording session. He guides the musicians, checks the decisions of the engineer, and is sometimes the arranger of the music.

The **Musician**, besides playing or singing, can offer suggestions to the arranger or director and helps contribute to the distinctive sound of the recording.

The **Tape Editor**, who is sometimes the same person as the Studio Engineer, is in charge of splicing (cutting) the tape of the final performance. If there is more than one track (for example, if the instrumental and vocal are recorded separately), the tape editor mixes the tracks and adjusts the sound levels. It is up to the Music Director to approve the finished product, so that the engineer and director often work together.

The **Tape Librarian** is responsible for storing the tapes. This person must maintain an accurate filing system which will make it possible to locate quickly any tape requested.

112

Listen to portions of a recording session done in Nashville, Tennessee. The musicians were recording the rock version of "Greensleeves." You will hear the Music Director, who is also the arranger, discussing the effects he wants. The musicians suggest improvisations for the introduction and ending of the song. At this session, the musicians played an important role in contributing details of the arrangement.

Develop a recording session

1. Prepare a musical arrangement to tape-record. (You might use ideas found on pages 32-33, 48-50, 110-11).
2. Decide what type of personnel you will need, and choose jobs.
3. Rehearse the arrangement.
4. Record the arrangement. Do several "takes" until you get a satisfactory result.

Music of the Pacific World

The Pacific World includes Japan, China, Korea, India, the countries of Indochina, and many island groups. Each nation has its own folk traditions which are reflected in its music.

The history of Eastern music is much older than that of the West. As early as the seventh century B.C., Chinese composers were creating music for ensembles of a thousand musicians. Music composed for religious and state ceremonies many centuries ago can still be heard in theaters and temples of the Orient.

Western music has also become popular in the East. In major cities, one can hear orchestras and soloists performing music by Western composers. The young people of the East enjoy Western popular music.

Eastern music has, in turn, influenced music of the West. In recent years Western composers have become aware of the interest and complexity of Eastern music. They have borrowed scales, rhythms, and musical forms for their own compositions. Some musicians have become fascinated with instruments native to the East, such as the Indian **sitar** and the Japanese **koto**.

As you study the music of different Pacific nations, try to identify the distinctive musical sounds of each. Think about how the language of a country influences the sound of its music. Listen to the music of composers who have tried to combine the traditions of East and West in their music. In the art section, notice the examples of visual art from this part of the world.

Greeting Song *(Salidommay)*

Kalingan Folk Song
English Words Adapted

Kalinga is a mountain province in the Philippines. The words of the first verse of this song are Kalingan expressions of joy. Study the design. How is it different from other songs you know? Tap the rhythm. What interesting patterns do you find? On what scale is the melody based? Do you know songs from another part of the world that are based on the same scale?

1. Dong - dong   ay ___   i - dong   i - lay,
2. Let   us   greet ___   our   guest   to - day,
3. He   came   to ___   us   from   Ma - ni - la,

In - sa - li - dom - may   di - - way,
In - sa - li - dom - may   di - - way,
In - sa - li - dom - may   di - - way,

I - la   i - la   i - la - lay,
I - la   i - la   i - la - lay,
I - la   i - la   i - la - lay,

In   sa - li - dom - may   di - - way.
Let   us   greet ___   our   guest   to - - day.
He   came   to ___   us   from   Ma - ni - la.

Arirang

Korean Folk Song
Words Adapted

1. A - ri - rang,__ A - ri - rang,__ A - ri - rang,__ A - ri - rang,__
2. A - ri - rang,__ A - ri - rang,__ A - ri - rang,__ A - ri - rang,__

A - ri - rang,__ A - ri - rang,__ A - ri - rang fair.
A - ri - rang,__ A - ri - rang,__ A - ri - rang fair.

Through the pass___ I watch you __ go __ there._____
Here I wait for you, wait, wait __ and __ stare._____

A - ri - rang,__ A - ri - rang,__ A - ri - rang fair.
A - ri - rang,__ A - ri - rang,__ A - ri - rang fair.

117

The Purple Bamboo

Chinese Folk Song

When you know the song, add the percussion accompaniment suggested on the next page. Someone might play the melody on a flute or recorder.

1. See I bring to you pur - ple bam - boo shoot,
2. You must try and grow like the bam - boo tall,

Now 'twill make a love - ly flute;
Then those part - ing lips so small

But those lips so small Can - not play at all
Soon will play the flute Made from bam - boo shoot;

On a love - ly gold - en ___ flute.
Sil - v'ry tunes will gent - ly ___ fall.

Refrain

Ee - tee - tee, Soon will come the hap - py

1. day. 2. day. My son the flute will play.

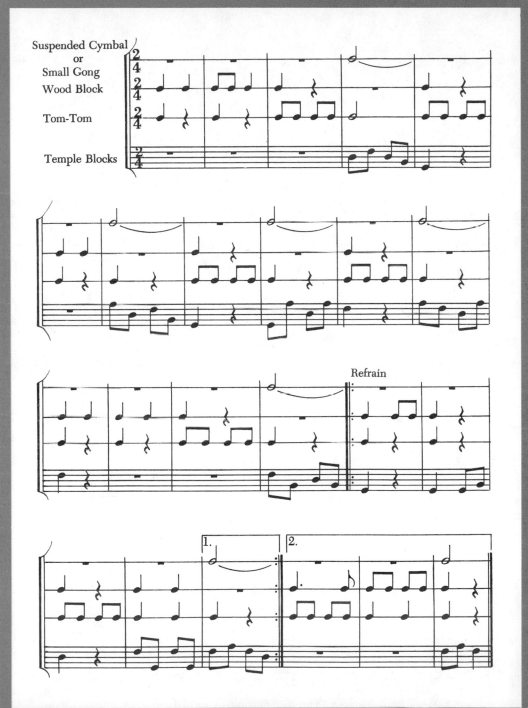

Flower Drum Song

Feng Yang Drum

Chinese Folk Song
English Words Adapted

Many Chinese folk songs are based on **pentatonic** scales. Here are two examples of the scale.

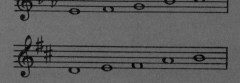

Play the two scales. How are they alike? How are they different?

Define a pentatonic scale.

Plan an accompaniment for this song using the instruments you played to accompany "The Purple Bamboo."

I ___ play a drum, she ___ plays a gong.

Play-ing the drum and gong we sing ___ a ___ song.

No oth - er song do we ev - er, ev - er sing.

We sing the Feng Yang song ___ all ___ day ___ long.

Feng Yang,— Feng Yang song,— here is how it's sung:

Refrain

Drr! Lin Tin Piak Ik Piak. Drr! Lin Tin Piak Ik Piak.

Drr Piak! Drr Piak! Drr Piak Drr Piak Piak Yeu Drr

Piak Piak Piak Ik Piak!

ancient chinese temple music

The Chinese musical culture is ancient and had its origin in traditions which began centuries before the time of Christ. Review the discussion on page 113. Then listen to the example of Chinese temple music on your recording. Notice the changing instrumental tone colors, an important element in Chinese musical compositions. You will hear a number of percussion instruments: high-pitched metal bells, cymbals, and drums of different sizes. A **hsaio** (flute), plays the high melody. Another tone color is added by the **seh,** a kind of harp.

And the Fallen Petals

by Chou Wen-chung

Music of every culture changes with the times. Listen to this music by Chou Wen-chung, a composer who was born in China and now lives in the United States. His music blends qualities of Eastern and Western cultures.

The title of this composition is taken from a poem by a Chinese poet of the eighth century:

All through the night
Such noise of wind and rain
And the fallen petals
Who knows how many!

The section of the composition on your recording is described by the composer: "A storm breaks and the furious wind drives the dazed petals far and wide."

As you listen, discuss elements you hear in the music which you feel have been influenced by Chinese musical culture. What in the music reflects Western musical traditions?

122

Lullaby

Vietnamese Folk Song
English Words Adapted

In this song, notice that you sing more than one pitch on some of the syllables. The Vietnamese often improvise similar patterns as they sing. This is common in this part of the world. What is distinctive about the rhythm of the song? What is distinctive about the design?

Rest your head,— Close your eyes dear one, Sleep, sleep, sleep.

Let pleas-ant dreams de - scend now, Sleep, sleep, sleep lit-tle child.—

Dark — is the sky sur - round - ing, Lit - tle one,

Sleep, sleep, sleep; You will wak - en in the morn - ing,

Strong, hap - py, well — rest - ed. — Sleep now, sleep,—

Close your eyes and dream — now, — Sleep,— sleep!

Weaving Dance

Indian Folk Song
English Words Adapted

This Indian dance is similar to the maypole dances of England. The dancers move around a pole from which hangs colored ribbons. As they dance, they weave the ribbons into a pattern.

Western melodies are based on scales. Indian melodies are based on **ragas**. The **raga** indicates the pitches to be used and also the melody patterns to be played. Listen to the **raga** played on the **sitar** on your recording.

Indian rhythm patterns are known as **talas**. This song is based on the **adi tala** which has eight beats. As you sing, clap the beats marked with accents:
1 2 3 4 5 6 7 8.
>   >   >

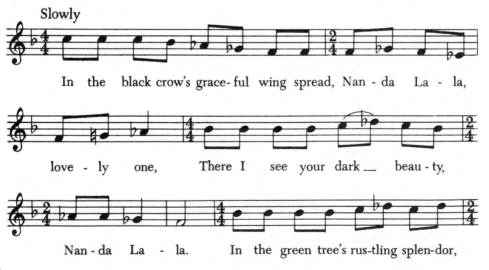

Slowly

In   the   black crow's grace-ful wing spread, Nan - da   La - la,

love - ly   one,   There I   see your dark __ beau - ty,

Nan - da   La - la.   In   the green tree's rus-tling splen-dor,

124

Nan - da La - la, I see there a - gain your beau-ty,

Nan - da La___ la.

Ragupati Ragava Rajah Ram

Hindu Hymn

In Hindu mythology, Ram is one of the names for God. This chant names Ram by several of his titles.

How much of the melody can you sing with "loo"? After you have practiced, listen to the recording to learn the words. Discover how the song is traditionally sung with leader and chorus. What happens during the last repetition of the refrain?

Ra - gu - pa - ti ra - ga - va ra - jah___ Ram _____

Puh - ti - ta bha - va - na si - ta - ram.

1. Si - ta - ram je si - ta - - ram,
2. Is - here Al - lah te - re ___ nam,

puh - ti - ta bha - va - na si - ta - ram. ram.
tub - ko sun mut - ti de bha - ga - wan. wan.

Suliram

Indonesian Folk Song

This Indonesian lullaby shows many Western musical characteristics. Over three hundred years ago the Portuguese and Dutch came to Indonesia. The Indonesians learned their songs and used some of the ideas to create new folk music of their own.

The words mean: "Suliram, the sweet Suliram, hush my baby; look there, my sweet baby. Now the sun rises very high. I see a water buffalo slain. For a long time I have looked for you. And now I have found you."

Su - li - ram, su - - li - ram, ram, ram, Su - li -

ram yang___ ma - nis, ___ A - du - hai in -

dung ___ se o - rang, ___ Bi - djak la sa - na di

pan - dang ma - nis. La su - li - nis.

Ting - i la ting - i, si ma - ta - ha - ri. Su - li - ram.

A - nak - lah ker - bau ma - ti ter - tam - bat. Su - li - ram.

Su - dah - lah la - ma sai - ya____ men - cha - ri. ____

D.S. al Fine

Ba - ru se ka - rang sai - ya____ men - da - pat. La su - li -

Gambangan

Listen to the music of a Balinese **gamelan,** or orchestra. The variety of instruments and complexity of music rivals the orchestras of the Western world. The gamelan includes a wide variety of percussion instruments. There are metallophones, pitched instruments made of metal, gongs of many sizes, drums, small cymbals, bells, and xylophones.

Listen to "Gambangan," and notice the many tone qualities the instruments produce. Try to identify the instruments. Listen again, and notice the music's design. Each group of instruments has a special role. The large metallophones play the basic melody while small ones play variations. Two small two-headed drums set the tempo. Other patterns are played on pitched bamboo rattles. The end of each phrase is marked by a deep-voiced gong.

127

East Wind

Japanese Folk Song

O East-wind, gent - ly blow-ing from O - bo - ne, Blow

sev - en long days or more! Do not cease, but in -

crease blow - ing, ___ To give fresh ___ meas - ure of breeze for our

treas - ured rice to please ___ all, When we

reap a boun - teous har - vest in ___ the ___ fall.

Tanko Bushi

Japanese Coal Miner's Dance

Listen to the music of this dance sung and played by Japanese musicians. What characteristics of Oriental music do you hear? How many phrases do you hear? Are they all the same length?

The dance imitates the work rhythm of coal miners. Practice the basic step for the dance. Learn the four movements. Sing "yoi-yoi" when it is heard at the end of the first and fourth phrases. Clap with the instrumental interlude.

Japanese court orchestras are another important part of Japanese music. Below is a picture of Japanese Imperial Court musicians playing the *san-no-tsuzumi,* the *biwa,* and the *sho.*

Music of Africa and the Middle East

The musical examples in this unit come from countries covering a wide geographic area. The Middle East includes Turkey, Saudi Arabia, Israel, Iraq, and Iran. Egypt, Libya, and Algeria are in Northern Africa. South of the Sahara are many African nations, some of which have gained independence only recently.

Western culture owes much to the Middle East and Northern Africa. To the best of our knowledge, civilization began there, and with the birth of civilization came the beginnings of music. The earliest records indicate that music was an important part of the first cultures. What other traditions, customs, and skills have we inherited from these ancient peoples?

To the African people, music is an essential part of daily life. It is used more frequently and spontaneously than it is in Western cultures. The young child might learn about his world from the songs his mother sings to him. Work songs, ceremonial songs, love songs, and epics have been handed down through many generations.

Visual art is also important in African culture. Find the examples of African art on page 232 of the art section. How is the music of Africa similar to its art?

Üsküdar

Turkish Folk Song
English Words Adapted

Üsküdar refers to a lush green region in the mountains of Turkey. The Turkish people sometimes accompany their vocal music with hand clapping or with a tambourine. The accompaniment is usually played on the accented beats.

1. On my way to Üs - kü - dar, it
2. On my way to Üs - kü - dar, I
3. I was look - ing for __ my __ love when

start - ed pour - ing rain. I was with my
found a hand - ker - chief, And a small piece
I found him be - side me. He be - longs to

dear __ be - lov - ed whose __ cape __ got __ all __
of __ sweet __ can - dy wrapped __ up __ in - side __
me and I be - long to him, that's __ all that mat - ters to __

1.
wet.
it.
me.

2.
wet.
it.
me.

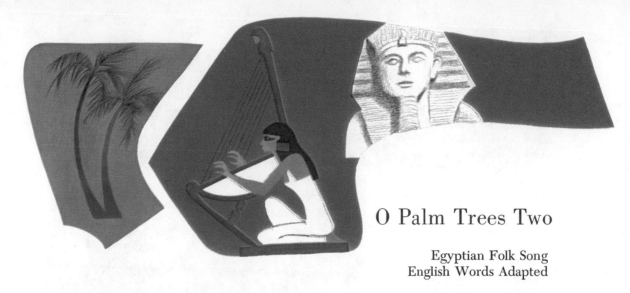

O Palm Trees Two

Egyptian Folk Song
English Words Adapted

Discuss the words. Why might Egyptians sing with such affection for the palm trees?

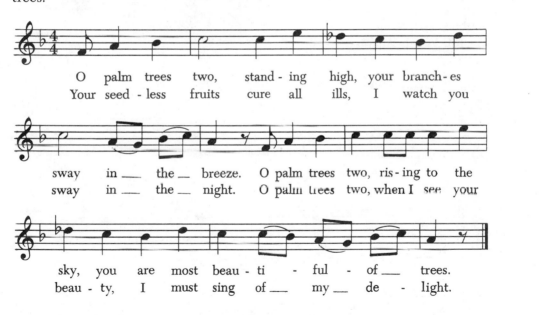

O palm trees two, stand-ing high, your branch-es
Your seed-less fruits cure all ills, I watch you

sway in __ the __ breeze. O palm trees two, ris-ing to the
sway in __ the __ night. O palm trees two, when I see your

sky, you are most beau-ti - ful - of __ trees.
beau-ty, I must sing of __ my __ de - light.

Lyres, harps, and other string instruments can be seen in the **friezes** of ancient Egyptian tombs. Pluck this pattern on a string instrument to suggest an accompaniment on one of these ancient instruments. The pattern uses the same pitches as the song.

The Caravan

Arabian Folk Song
English Words Adapted

Add an accompaniment on tambourine and finger cymbals.

On the des - ert, pa - tient _ cam - els la - den with spi - ces and

gold, Tread - ing soft - ly on deep _ car - pets of

sand just as in days of old. Li - li - li - li - li the _

driv - ers sing. Ding - a - ling - a - ling the _ cam - el bells ring.

"Sa - u - ni, move on - ward," The car - a - van must go on. "Sa - u - ni, move swift - ly," Be - fore the day is gone. Li - li - li - li - li the __ driv - ers sing. Ding - a - ling - a - ling hear the cam - el bells ring.

Notice that this song uses only five tones. Is it like other pentatonic songs you have sung? Play the melody on the xylophone. Improvise other melodies using the same five tones.

Tum Balalyka

Jewish Folk Song
Words by Ruth Robbins

Follow the suggestions on pages 11 and 22, and learn the song. Be sure to examine both voice parts in the refrain as you give your answers. Compare the melody of the verse and refrain. What similarities and differences do you discover that will help you learn the song?

Is the harmonized refrain an example of polyphony or homophony? Can you add harmony to the verse?

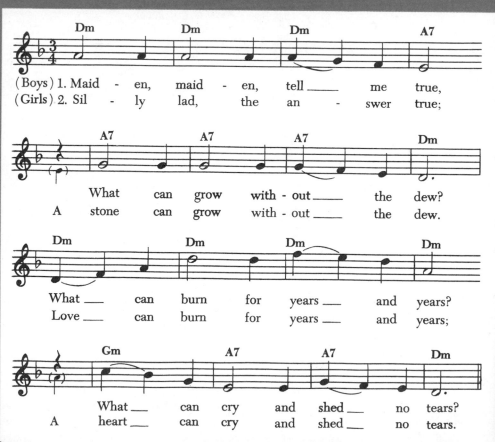

(Boys) 1. Maid - en, maid - en, tell ___ me true,
(Girls) 2. Sil - ly lad, the an - swer true;

What can grow with - out ___ the dew?
A stone can grow with - out ___ the dew.

What ___ can burn for years ___ and years?
Love ___ can burn for years ___ and years;

What ___ can cry and shed ___ no tears?
A heart ___ can cry and shed ___ no tears.

Tzena, Tzena

Words by Mitchell Parish
Music by I. Miron and J. Grossman

Tze - na, Tze - na, Tze - na, Tze - na, How can an - y-
Tze - na, Tze - na, Tze - na, Tze - na, Don't you know your

thing be plain - er than ____ my love for you? ____
eyes con - tain a look ____ that thrills me through? __

Refrain

Tze - na, Tze - na, ev - ery - one is wait - ing,
Ev - ery - one is hap - py cel - e - brat - ing,

For a wed- ding they're an - ti - ci - pat - ing,
Peo - ple danc - ing in the streets! __

Clap your hands and (clap) raise your voic-es high-er, Make a cir-cle
Dance the Ho-ra (clap) to your heart's de-sire,— All the world's in

while we dance a-round the fire, — love with Tze-na, Tze-na.

The people of Israel have immigrated to their new nation from all over the world. Each group has brought their own music with them. Other songs have been newly written to tell of life in the new land. Compare the style of "Tzena, Tzena" with "Tum Balalyka" and "Shalom Alëhem."

Study the design of the song. How many sections do you find? Notice that each section is to be repeated.

When you know the melody, create harmony by singing the song as a two-part round. Group two should enter when group one begins to sing section two. Later, try singing the song as a three-part round.

Shalom Alëḥem

Jewish Folk Song

The words of this Hebrew song mean "Peace be with you."

140

Prayer for Africa

Bwana Ibariki Afrika

Words and Music by Enoch Sontonga

This lovely prayer is sung by many African people of different nations. It is written for you to sing in English and Swahili.

With dignity

Bless, O Lord, our coun - try, Af - ri - ca,
Bwa - na, i - ba - ri - ki Af - ri - ka,

So that she may wak - en from her sleep.
I - li - i - pa - te ___ ku - am - ka.

Fill her horn with plen - ty, guide her feet.
Ma - om - bi ye to ya - si - ki - lel.

Hear us, faith - ful ___ sons.
U - tu - ba - ri - ki.

Spir - it, Spir - it,
U - je, U - je,

Spir - it, de - scend, ___
U - je Ro - ho, ___

D.S. with repeat

Spir - it, de - scend, Spir - it, de - scend, Spir - it di - vine.
U - je Ro - ho, U - je Ro - ho, U - ta - ja - ze.

Spirit Song

African Folk Song
English Words Adapted

The spirit song was probably part of an ancient ceremony. Learn to sing each of the three sections; pay careful attention to the changing meters and differences in tempo.

When you know the individual sections, combine them into one long song. Each section may be repeated as often as you wish. While some sing, others may dance, and a third group may add an accompaniment. During the first section play:

During the second section play:

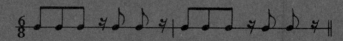

142

African dancers often move in a circle or line formation. They may choose an animal symbol to guide their dance creation. With arms held out to suggest the wings of a bird, develop a stepping pattern that moves in an even rhythm, grouped in twos or threes. Be sure to keep your groupings so that you feel your own meter against the changing meter of the melody.

Add an accompaniment using body sounds. Experiment with different ways of making these sounds: clapping, stamping, tongue-clacking, and slapping knees, chest, or upper arms. Notice the different qualities of sound. Develop a rhythm pattern that moves in groups of six eighth notes. As your accompaniment is repeated over and over, notice the interesting **cross rhythms** created between the even metric groupings of the accompaniment and the uneven metric groupings of the song.

143

Nana Kru

Liberian Folk Song

This amusing wedding song tells of certain customs which are common when young couples marry in Africa. Does the rhythm remind you of any songs you know from the Western world?

Add this accompaniment on the drum.

Na- na,   Na - na Kru,   Na - na,   Na - na, Na - na

Kru,   Jump in - to my ca - noe, ___

Na - na,   I paid my dow-ry for   you.

Na - na, Na - na, Na - na, Na - na, Na - na Kru, Na - na Kru,

Na - na, Na - na, Na - na, Na - na Kru,   Na - na Kru,

Jump in - to my ca - noe, ___   Na - na,   I paid my dow-ry for

you.   I saw your ma,   And I saw your pa,   I

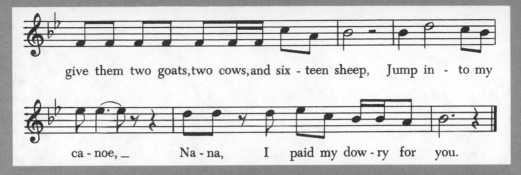

give them two goats, two cows, and six - teen sheep, Jump in - to my

ca - noe, __ Na - na, I paid my dow - ry for you.

Everybody Loves Saturday Night

Mofe Moni S'mo Ho Gbeke

African Folk Song

All over the world Saturday night is a night for recreation. Versions of this song are enjoyed in many sections of West Africa. Learn to sing it in English; then listen to the recording and learn the words in the *Ga* language.

1.
Ev- ery- bod - y   loves   Sat - ur - day   night. _____
Mo- fe mo - ni   s'mo   ho ___ gbe - ke. _____

2.
Ev- ery- bod - y   loves   Sat - ur - day   night. _____
Mo- fe mo - ni   s'mo   ho ___ gbe - ke. _____

3.
Ev-ery-bod-y,   ev-ery-bod-y,   ev-ery-bod-y,   ev-ery-bod-y,
Mo-fe mo-ni,   mo-fe mo-ni,   mo-fe mo-ni,   mo-fe mo - ni,

4.
Ev - ery - bod - y   loves   Sat - ur - day night. _____
Mo - fe mo - ni   s'mo   ho ___ gbe - ke. _____

MUSIC OF NIGERIA

Nigeria is a large country, divided into four regions. Each region has a main tribe, special customs, and a major language. Yet within any one region there may be many differences in living patterns. These variations are reflected in the music.

There are work songs which are often short and repetitive, with a chorus responding to the soloist. Listen to an example from Eastern Nigeria on your recording.

Other music has long, extended melodies, such as the marriage song from Northern Nigeria on your record. Notice that, in this music, the choir has its own important part, instead of just echoing the soloist. Listen to the drum and flute accompaniment.

The music of Nigeria, like the music of our own land, keeps changing to fit the changing customs. Here is an example of an ancient Yoruba religious song, from Western Nigeria. The words mean, "The sea pebble is immortal; we too (as children of the god) have become immortal; we shall never die."

During the early days of Christianity in Nigeria, new words were set to the traditional melody, altering it to suit the demands of the Yoruba tone-language. Listen to this version; notice similarities and differences. The words mean, "God, our God, is great beyond comprehension; He is Immortal, the Ever-Living One; our God is Immortal."

Instrumental music is also an important part of Nigerian musical life. One of the traditional groups is the *dundun* orchestra. Listen to the explanation on your recording. Here are some of the patterns you will hear.

Iya Ilu (mother drum)

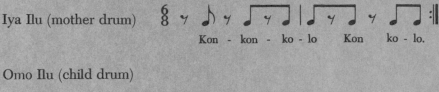

Kon - kon - ko - lo   Kon   ko - lo.

Omo Ilu (child drum)

Gudugudu:

Pe - pe - pe - pe.

Experiment with these drum patterns. Each is a reproduction of a phrase from the Yoruba tone-language. When you can play the patterns, try combining them to form your own orchestra. Another time make up drum patterns based on phrases from your language.

Today people travel easily from one land to another; they meet people of many cultures and learn each other's customs through books, recordings, and television. Many times, ideas and customs from one culture are absorbed into another. This blending of traditions can often be heard in music of our time. Listen to the final example on your recording. It is a composition by a Yoruba composer, Fela Sowande, who now lives in the United States. Listen to "Akinla" from *African Suite*. It is a "marriage" of Yoruba traditional music, Nigerian Highlife or popular music, Afro-American jazz, and European composed music.

147

Manamolela

South African Work Song
English Lyrics by Pete Seeger

This is an example of **antiphonal** singing. The leader begins a melodic phrase. Before he finishes, the chorus echoes him. Learn the song in unison by following the instructions on pages 11 and 22. Then choose one person to be the leader. Notice the interesting harmony which occurs when the voices are combined.

148

You know the day is long. Ma - na - mo -

day is long, You know the day is long.

le - la, Ma - na - mo - le - - - -

Won't you let us take it slow? Won't you let us

la, Won't you let us take it slow? Won't you let us

take it slow? You know the day is long, ____

take it slow? You know the day is long, ___

___ You know the day is long.___

___ You know the day is long.

Music of Latin America

The vast area known as Latin America is rich in contrasts — of typography, climate, and resources. Latin America includes Mexico, the countries of Central America, the islands of the Caribbean, and the big farm-countries of South America.

The music of this region is as full of contrasts as the land. The folk music blends Indian, African, and Spanish influences. The native Indians contributed plaintive, slow-moving melodies, often based on ancient pentatonic scales. In the music of the Caribbean, we find rhythms that were brought to the New World by the Africans. From Spain came flowing melodies, simple harmonies, and intricate dance rhythms.

Because so many Latin Americans have moved to the United States, Latin music and customs are familiar to us. Many communities in the Southwest observe traditional Latin American celebrations. Latin music has influenced popular music of today. Some of our dances, such as the tango and the samba, are based on dance rhythms from South America.

As you study the music in this unit, try to identify some of the features that might have originated in Spain or Africa. Discover how these influences contribute to the special sound of Latin American music.

Chiapanecas

Mexican Folk Song
English Words Adapted

With spirit

There's a song they know __ down in Mex - i - co; __

__ Ev - ery - one seems to sing Chia - pa - ne - cas.

It's an eas - y thing, __ once you feel the swing; __

__ Sim - ply let your - self go, Chia - pa - ne - cas.

Now then sing a - long __ with this hap - py song, __

Sing a - - long, __

__ And you'll soon feel the hol - i - day spir - it!

Join us as we go __ to old Mex - i - co, __

And en - joy the fi - es - ta, O - lé!

So, Sing Chia - pa - ne - cas, O - lé,
Join in the fun, sing O - lé, O - lé,

Say Chia - pa - ne - cas, O - lé, O - lé!

Dance, dance, ev - ery - one's danc - ing; Sing, sing,
dance, dance, join in the danc - ing; Mex - i -

ev - ery - one's sing - ing; Sway, sway, ev - ery - one's
co's, for ro - manc - ing; Come now, let your - self

1.
feel - ing gay! _____ Come a - long now and
go and _____

2.
sing Chia - pa - ne - cas, O - lé. O - lé!

¡Temporal! (Hurricane)

Puerto Rican Folk Song
English Words Adapted

This song tells of the dreaded hurricanes which often threaten the lives of the island people. Warnings are passed on by word of mouth as people prepare to evacuate. When they return to their homes, they may find little remaining.

Boys, read the part written in the bass clef. Girls, sing the part written in the treble clef.

La vidalita

South American Cowboy Song
Arranged by Kurt Miller
Words Adapted by Kurt Miller

1. Ev - ery - day I ride, cross - ing prai - ries wide,
2. Night with star - ry light, at the camp - fire bright,

Ah, _____ La, La Vi - da - li - ta.

(Melody)

La Vi - da - li - ta, sí!

(Melody)

(1.) Cat - tle mill - ing 'round, dust clouds hide the ground,
(2.) Noth - ing stirs the air, peace is ev - ery - where,

1.

2.

Ah, _____ La, La Vi - da - li - ta. La Vi - da - li - ta.

(Melody)

La Vi - da - li - ta, sí! sí!

Trinidad

Words and Music
by Massie Patterson and Sammy Heyward

Follow the instructions on page 11, and learn the rhythm of this song. Clap the syncopated patterns. What causes syncopation in rhythm?

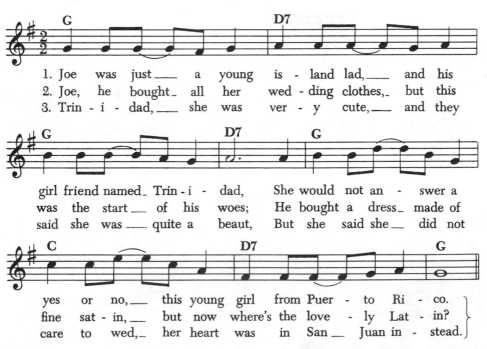

1. Joe was just __ a young is - land lad, __ and his
2. Joe, he bought __ all her wed - ding clothes, __ but this
3. Trin - i - dad, __ she was ver - y cute, __ and they

girl friend named __ Trin - i - dad, She would not an - swer a
was the start __ of his woes; He bought a dress __ made of
said she was __ quite a beaut, But she said she __ did not

yes or no, __ this young girl from Puer - to Ri - co.
fine sat - in, __ but now where's the love - ly Lat - in?
care to wed, __ her heart was in San __ Juan in - stead.

Refrain

Trin-i-dad,— oh Trin-i-dad,— please, my dar-ling, don't
act so mean,— Please come back — to me,
ain't it plain— to see, I will make— you my queen.

PLAY CALYPSO RHYTHMS

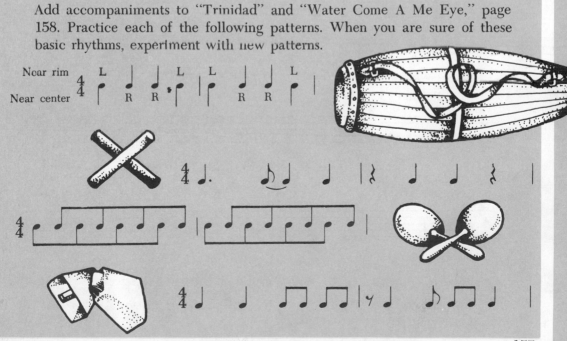

Add accompaniments to "Trinidad" and "Water Come A Me Eye," page 158. Practice each of the following patterns. When you are sure of these basic rhythms, experiment with new patterns.

Near rim
Near center

Water Come A Me Eye

Jamaican Folk Song
Words Adapted

Moderately slow

1. Ev - ery time I think of Li - za
2. Don't know why you went a - way, ___
3. Time go slow when love is past, ___
4. Lis - ten 'cause I'm call - in' you, ___

Wa - ter come a me eye. Ev - ery time I
Wa - ter come a me eye. When you com - in'
Wa - ter come a me eye. When you come back,
Wa - ter come a me eye. And my heart is

think of Li - za Wa - ter come a me eye.
home to stay? ___ Wa - ter come a me eye.
time go fast, ___ Wa - ter come a me eye.
call - in' too, ___ Wa - ter come a me eye.

Refrain

Come back, Li - za, come back girl, Wa - ter come a me eye.

Come back, Li - za, come back girl, Wa - ter come a me eye.

MUSIC FOR THE STEEL BAND

Listen to "Yellow Bird" played by a steel band from the Caribbean. Notice also the rhythmic accompaniment, typical of calypso music, played on drums, cymbals, and cowbells.

You can make your own steel drums.

1. Collect some one-gallon cans. Gently punch the end into a concave shape with a ¾" dowel stick and a mallet.
2. Turn the can over and set it on the open end of another can approximately the size of a frozen juice can. Place this can to one side of the depressed end.
3. Tap from the inside of the larger can and gradually make a small depression over the smaller can. Test this "bubble" for its pitch by turning over the can and tapping it.
4. Use a second open-ended can, one slightly larger than the juice can, to make another bubble. The pitch of this bubble should be slightly lower. Test it as you make it.
5. You may use cans of other sizes to produce more "steel drums." See how many different pitches you can make. Paint the names of the pitch on the bubble. Use these cans separately, or join them to form a larger steel drum. Experiment with a variety of mallets to produce a desirable sound.

Viva Jujuy

Argentinian Folk Song
Arranged and Adapted by Theodore Bikel and Geula Gill

Vi - va Ju - juy, — vi - va la Pu - na, Vi - va mi a - ma

da. Vi - van los cer - ros, Pin - ta ra - jea - dos De mi que - bra -

da. da. De mi que - bra - da,

Hu - ma - hua - que - ña. No te se - pa - res

De mis a - mo - res Tu eres mi due - ña.

Dansa

from *Bachianas
Brasileiras No. 4*

by Heitor Villa-Lobos

Review the Spanish and Latin American music you have learned. Then listen
to "Dansa" by the Brazilian composer Villa-Lobos. Does this music seem
to share characteristics with other music you have learned?
The first section is based on a theme played in the middle range of the
piano. Listen for repetitions of this theme. Are they exact or varied? Notice
changes in dynamics. How many sections do you hear?

In My Spacious Palace

Folk Song from Ecuador
English Words Adapted

Long before the Spanish arrived in the New World, there were highly developed civilizations in Central and South America. The people of these cultures gave music an important place in their ceremonies. This song is from the Quechas, one of the groups who formed the Inca Empire. Compare the music with other Latin American music.

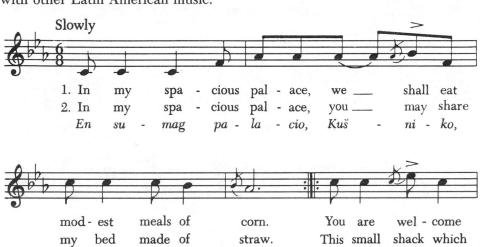

Slowly

1. In my spa - cious pal - ace, we ___ shall eat
2. In my spa - cious pal - ace, you ___ may share
   En su - mag pa - la - cio, Kuš - ni - ko,

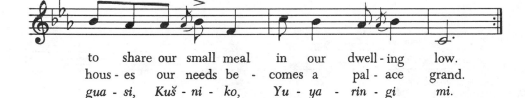

mod - est meals of corn. You are wel - come
my bed made of straw. This small shack which
Kau - sa - xun - gi mi; Ño - ka čag - ľa

to share our small meal in our dwell - ing low.
hous - es our needs be - comes a pal - ace grand.
gua - si, Kuš - ni - ko, Yu - ya - rin - gi mi.

Naranjita (The Golden Orange)

Folk Song from Ecuador

This song comes from the same country as "In My Spacious Palace." Do you find any Indian influences in this music? Do you find any characteristics of Spanish music?

Lively

Na - ran - ji - ta,   pin - ta, pin - ti - ta,

Te he de ro - bar de tu quin - ta   Si - no es es - ta no - che - ci - ta

Ma - ña - na por la ma - ña - ni - ta,   ta.

Na - ran - ji - ta,   pin - ta, pin - ti - ta,

pin - ta, pin - ti - ta.

As an introduction, begin with this rhythm on a small drum.

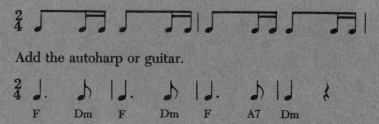

Add the autoharp or guitar.

162

Folk Music of Latin America

Latin American music is a blend of many cultures: Indian, African, Portuguese, and Spanish. Discuss reasons why this has happened.

Listen to "Oígame Juanita" from Ecuador. You will hear drums, bamboo flutes, and instruments made from gourds. You will also hear sounds made by blowing on a leaf held between the hands. The melody is similar to other Indian melodies. Where might the rhythms have come from?

Now listen to "El mariachi" played by a mariachi band. These bands originated in Mexico a hundred years ago. The first ones included a guitar, violin, and trumpet or clarinet. Modern bands have added several guitars of different sizes and a bass viol. This music has been primarily influenced by the music of Spain.

Panambí

Invocation of the Powerful Spirits

Lament of the Maidens

by Alberto Ginastera

Latin American composers have helped their people gain pride in their heritage by writing music based on themes from national history. Listen to music from "Panambí," a ballet based on an ancient legend. The composer, Ginastera, is from Argentina.

Listen first to "Invocation of the Powerful Spirits," performed by percussion instruments and brass. How many different percussion instruments can you identify? Which brass instruments are heard?

"Lament of the Maidens" is based on two melodic ideas. The first is stated by the strings, the second by a solo flute. Draw the melodic contour of each pattern. Then listen to the entire movement, and notice how they are repeated, altered, and varied.

Pollerita

Bolivian Folk Song
English Words Adapted

Very fast

Po - lle - ri - ta, po - lle - ri - ta de mi cho - li - ta,
Po - lle - ri - ta, lit - tle skirt the col - or of ros - es,

Po - lle - ri - ta, po - lle - ri - ta co - lor ro - si - ta;
Po - lle - ri - ta, po - lle - ri - ta of my Cho - li - ta;

¡Qué bien te bai - las, qué bien te can - tas
Watch how she dan - ces while she is sing - ing

Con mi cha - ran - gui - to! ¡Qué bien te bai - las,
To my — lit - tle gui - tar. Watch how she dan - ces

1st Time **To Refrain**

qué bien te can - tas Con mi cha - ran - gui - to!
while she is sing - ing To my — lit - tle gui - tar.

2nd Time **To** ⊕

¡Con la lla - me - ra - da.
To my lla - me - ra - da.

164

Con mi che - ran - gui - to! _____ Yah! _
To my __ little gui - tar! _____ Yah! _

Refrain

Sa - ra ma - la - gu ta tu, Ma - na tri - go pe - la - cu,
She shall nev - er do the chores, Husk the bar - ley, wash the floors,

Ma - na chu - ño pun - ti - co. Sa - ra ma - la - gu ta tu,
This for her is not to do. She shall nev - er do the chores,

Ma - na tri - go pe - la - cu, Ma - na chu - ño pun - ti - co.
Husk the bar - ley, wash the floors, I would rath - er watch her dance.

A mi no me gus - ta cu - lla - gua - das
Oh my lit - tle love - ly Cho - li - ta,

A mi si me gus - ta lla - me - ra - da. Ta - pic - a - pic - a - pic.
Lis - ten to her play the lla - me - ra - da. Ta - pic - a - pic - a - pic.

A mi no me gus - ta cu - lla - gua - das
Oh my lit - tle love - ly Cho - li - ta,

Back to Refrain

A mi si me gus - ta lla - me - ra - da.
Wear - ing now her ros - y po - lle - ri - ta.

165

More Music to Explore

You have studied music of many different times and places. You have discovered that the music of each country and period has its own character. You also discovered that the music of one country or period often influences that of another.

In this unit you will sing songs of your own country. As you learn these songs and review old favorites, discuss the musical characteristics that you find. Which are uniquely our own? Which show the influence of the music of other lands?

As you listen to twentieth-century compositions in this unit, try to identify musical ideas from earlier centuries. What types of musical organization seem to be completely new?

Try to imagine the kind of music that will be heard in the twenty-first century. Do you think people will be enjoying the same music one hundred years from now? What kinds of new musical explorations will be possible?

Sing

Words and Music
by Joe Raposo

good e - nough for an - y - one else to hear. Sing!

Sing a song! ___ La la do la da, La

da la do la da, La da da la do la la. ___

La do la da, La da la la da, Lo da da la do lo da. _

repeat and fade

___ ___ La la do la da, La

da la do la da, La da da la do la da. ___

Twelve-Bar Blues

Talk the blues.

Do you wan-na court your gal? Cash is spent!

Do you wan-na court your gal? Cash is spent!

Rob a Nash-ville bank, and the judge-'ll pay the rent!

In many blues verses, such as the one above, the first two lines are the same. The third line is a "surprise statement."

Try writing words for your own blues verse.

Blues harmony

There are twelve bars (measures) in these blues. Play the chord sequence outlined below. Use autoharp, guitar, or piano as you "talk" the blues.

First four bars—play the C chord:

| | **C** | 1 | 2 | 3 | 4 |
Do you wan-na court your gal? Cash is spent! Do you

For the next two bars—play the F chord: **F** | 5 | 6 |
wan-na court your gal?

For the next two bars—play the C chord: **C** | 7 | 8 |
Cash is spent!

Then play the G7 chord: **G7** | 9 | 10 |
Rob a Nash-ville bank, and the

and end with the C chord: **C** | 11 | 12 |
judge'll pay the rent!

Now try the same sequence of chords with your own blues verse.

170

Blues melody

A blues melody is based on the major scale, but two tones—the third and seventh—are often lowered.

Major scale .... Major scale with flat third and seventh

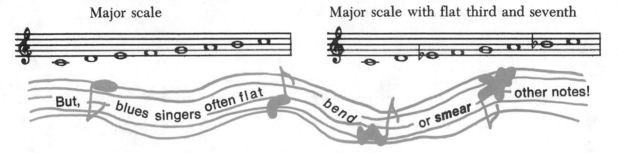

But, blues singers often flat bend or smear other notes!

These "flatted" tones sounding with the "non-flatted" tones in the harmony create tension in the blues.

Try making up a blues melody. Sing it, or play it on bells or piano.

Choose from these tones:

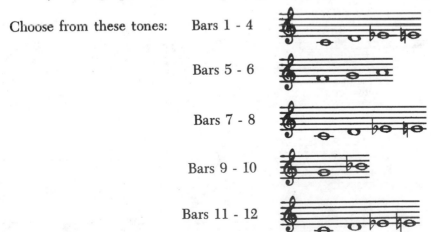

Bars 1 - 4

Bars 5 - 6

Bars 7 - 8

Bars 9 - 10

Bars 11 - 12

Put it together and add chords. Do you hear tension in your melody?
Now make up a melody for your own blues verse.

Consider Yourself

from Oliver!

Words and Music by Lionel Bart

Moderate march tempo

Con - sid - er your - self ____ at home, ____ Con -

sid - er your - self ____ one of the fam - i - ly. ____ I've

tak - en to you ____ so strong, ____ It's

clear we're go - ing to get a - long! Con -

sid - er your - self ____ well in, ____ Con -

sid - er your - self ____ part of the fur - ni - ture. ___ There

is - n't a lot ____ to spare; ____ Who

cares? What - ev - er we've got we share! { If it should
{ No - bod - y

chance to be, we should see some hard - er days,___ Emp - ty
tries to be lah - di - dah and up - pit - y,___ There's a

lard - er days,___ why grouse? ___ Al - ways a
cup o' tea ___ for all. ___ On - ly it's

chance we'll meet some - bod - y to foot the bill,___ Then the
wise, to be han - dy with a roll - ing pin ___ When the

drinks are on the house! ___ } Con -
land - lord comes to call! ___ }

sid - er your - self ___ our mate, ___ We

don't want to have ___ no fuss, ___ For

af - ter some con - sid - er - a - tion, we can state: Con -

sid - er your - self ___ one of us.

Talkin' Blues

The "blues" are melancholy songs from which American jazz drew many ideas. The Afro-American often sang blues songs as he worked in the fields or rested in the evening. This "talkin' blues" is to be chanted in a rhythmic "sing-song" while chords are strummed on the guitar, banjo, or autoharp.

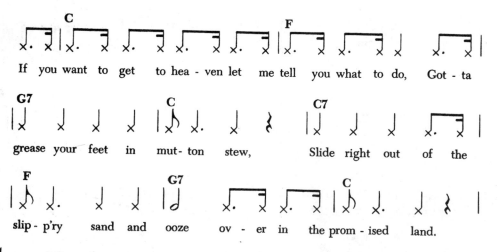

If you want to get to hea - ven let me tell you what to do, Got - ta
grease your feet in mut - ton stew, Slide right out of the
slip - p'ry sand and ooze ov - er in the prom - ised land.

Music of Now

Much music of today is a blend of the music from other times and places. As you listen to the musical examples shown on this "Tree of Music," talk about how one branch seems to have influenced another.

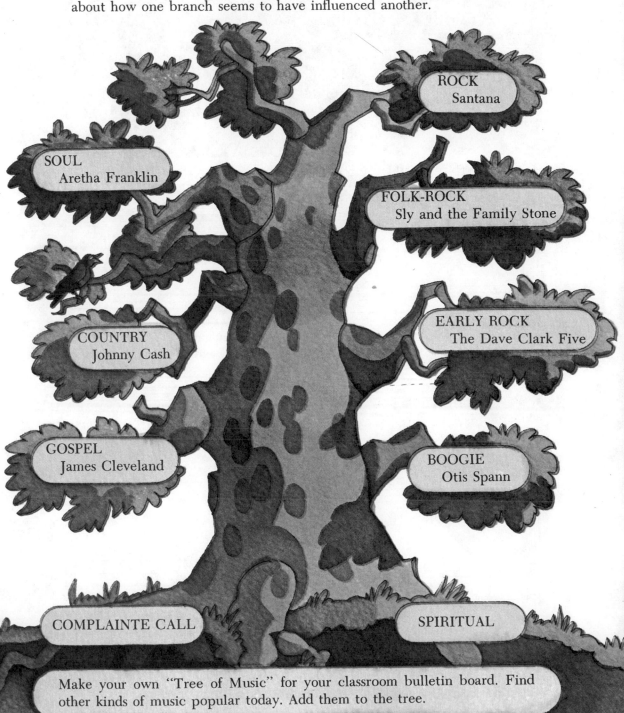

ROCK
Santana

SOUL
Aretha Franklin

FOLK-ROCK
Sly and the Family Stone

EARLY ROCK
The Dave Clark Five

COUNTRY
Johnny Cash

GOSPEL
James Cleveland

BOOGIE
Otis Spann

COMPLAINTE CALL

SPIRITUAL

Make your own "Tree of Music" for your classroom bulletin board. Find other kinds of music popular today. Add them to the tree.

Down by the Riverside

Spiritual
Arranged by Buryl Red

This song and "Talkin' Blues" come from the Afro-American tradition. After you have learned them, compare both with the music you have learned from Africa and the West Indies. What features do you find that are common to all? Do you find any musical characteristics in "Down by the Riverside" which show the influence of another culture?

stud - y war no more, __ oh

Stud - y war no more, __

stud - y war no more, __ I ain't gon - na

stud - y war no more, __

stud - y war no more, I ain't gon - na

no more,

stud - y war no more,

stud - y war no more, __ oh,

stud - y war no more, __

Compose Han Music

Hold your hands in front of you. What do you notice as you compare your two hands? Can you compose a melody that demonstrates the similarities and differences you noticed?

- The **direction** of your five-tone melody must match the contour formed by the tips of the fingers of your **left hand** when held upright, palm facing outward, away from you.

- Position your fingers exactly as shown in the picture (close-close-apart-close). The size of the interval between each tone must match the distance between each finger. Use two of the intervals shown in the chart—one to represent fingers close to each other and another to represent fingers far apart.

On a sheet of paper write the pitch names you will use.

Extend Your Melody

Let the direction and intervals match your **right hand**.

Direction: ?
Pitch name: ?
Interval size: ?

Now turn your left hand **upside down** with the palm **facing** you:
Direction: ?
Pitch name: ?
Interval: ?

Turn your **right hand** upside down with the palm **facing** you:
Direction: ?
Pitch name: ?
Interval: ?

Play your four melody patterns. What similarities do you notice? What differences?

Use your four patterns to create a setting for this poem.
You may use the patterns in any order you wish.
Consider the meaning of the poem as you decide the order of your pattern.

Shadows

The moon is risen, and without a sound
They write their welcome songs along the ground.

From *Japanese Poetry* by Curtis Hidden Page. Used by permisson of the estate of Curtis Hidden Page.

Play on Notes

Words and Music
by Milton Babbitt

This song is based on a twelve-tone row. Six of the tones are used in the voice part and six are used in the bell part. Can you discover how the composer has arranged his series? Does he use the four different arrangements you learned on page 181 as a guide?

This song is also a "play on words"! Can you decide why? Study the words carefully. Notice the note that appears above each word as it is repeated.

sound   the   note,   and   play   here.

Part II

Hear,   play,   and   note   the   sound;

sound   and   play   the   note   here.

Here   note   the   play   and   sound;

sound   the   note,   and   play   here.

The Night Piece

Music by Arthur Frackenpohl
Words by Robert Herrick

This poem was written by a man who lived in England during the Golden Age. Centuries later, a contemporary American composer set the words to music.

Compare the sound of this music to music of the Golden Age. Can you find any similarities? any differences?

Lullaby of the Sea

Music by
Arthur Frackenpohl
Words Anonymous

Quietly

1. Hush, the waves are roll - ing in, White with foam, white with foam;
2. Hush, the winds roar harsh and deep, On they come, on they come,
3. Hush, the rain sweeps o'er the knolls, Where they roam, where they roam;

Fa - ther toils a - mid the din, But ba - by sleeps at home.
Broth - er seeks the wan-d'ring sheep, But ba - by sleeps at home.
Sis - ter goes to seek the cows, But ba - by sleeps at home.

MUSIC IN THE TWENTIETH CENTURY

In the early twentieth century, composers began to explore new ways of organizing musical sounds. They felt the need to break away from traditional forms and to seek ways of composing which would better express the ideas and feelings of a new century.

Tone Roads No. 3

by Charles Ives

In traditional music we are accustomed to hearing each musical idea or voice support and interact with each other. In this music by Charles Ives, each strand of sound seems to continue on its own path without regard to the other sounds which make up the total. Instruments play in different meters, with different melodic and harmonic ideas. This music can be described as **atonal** because there is no consistent tonal center, or "home tone."

Three Poems by Henri Michaux

by Witold Lutoslawski

This composition, by a contemporary Polish composer, combines many of the experiments of twentieth-century composers. It is performed by two ensembles—one instrumental, the other vocal. Each has its own conductor. On the score, pitches are indicated, but at times their exact duration is left to the conductor and the performer. As a result, each performance is different. The type of music is sometimes called **chance music.** Listen to the composition. What twentieth-century musical ideas do you hear?

Six Pieces for Orchestra, Opus 6, First Piece

by Anton Webern

In traditional music, the design is a result of repetition and contrast of harmonic and melodic ideas. In twentieth-century music, the design is often the result of organizing additional musical elements such as tone color, dynamics, or texture.

Listen to Webern's music for orchestra. What element seems to be the organizing force in this music? To decide, listen for repetition of a specific element. Do you hear repetition of any melodic fragments? of rhythm patterns? of instrumental tone colors?

In Memoriam Dylan Thomas

Prelude

by Igor Stravinsky

Other composers have experimented with new means of tonal organization as the basis for their melodies and harmonies. The music is sometimes called serial because it is based on a series of pitches. The series of pitches is called a **tone row.** Review the discussion of serial music on page 181. Then listen to this short composition for solo voice and string and brass instruments. It is based on a five-tone row. Can you hear any of the transformations of the row?

The Inch Worm

Words and Music
by Frank Loesser

This song and the one on the next pages are from the movie, *Hans Christian Andersen*. Movies and plays which use music to help tell the story are known as **musical comedies**. This form has been developed by American composers. What other musical comedies do you know?

Slowly

Two and two are four, four and four are eight;

That's all you have on your busi - ness - like mind.

Two and two are four, four and four are eight;

How can you be so blind?_____

Refrain

Two and two are four, Four and four are eight,

Inch worm, inch worm, mea - sur - ing the mar - i - golds,

Eight and eight are six-teen, Six-teen and six-teen are thir-ty two.

You and your a - rith- me-tic, you'll prob-a - bly go far. _____

Two and two are four, Four and four are eight,

Inch worm, inch worm, mea - sur - ing the mar - i - golds,

Eight and eight are six - teen, Six - teen and six-teen are thir-ty two.

Seems to me you'd stop and see how beau-ti - ful they are.

Wonderful Copenhagen

Words and Music
by Frank Loesser
Arranged by William Stickles

Won - der - ful, won - der - ful Co - pen - ha - gen,

Won - der - ful, won - der - ful Co - pen - ha - gen,

friend - ly old girl of a town, _____ With her

friend - ly old girl of a town, _____

har - bor light, that she wears at night, Like a

Like a

gold - en, gold - en crown. _____ Oh,

gold - en, gold - en crown. _____ Oh,

190

won - der - ful, won - der - ful Co - pen - ha - gen,

won - der - ful, won - der - ful Co - pen - ha - gen,

sal - ty old queen of the sea, _____

sal - ty old queen of the sea, _____ Once I

Sing - ing

sailed a - way, but I'm home to - day, Sing - ing

Co - pen - ha - gen, won - der - ful, won - der - ful

Co - pen - ha - gen, won - der - ful, won - der - ful

Co - pen - ha - gen for me. _____

Co - pen - ha - gen for me. _____

Listen to Electronic Music

In the twentieth century one of the important musical developments has been electronic music. One of the first ways composers experimented with electronic composition was through the use of the tape recorder. Listen to Milton Babbitt, a composer of electronic music, explain some of the ways sounds can be transformed through the manipulation of the tape and tape recorder.

A Piece for Tape Recorder

by Vladimir Ussachevsky

This composition is included because it was one of the earliest created on the tape recorder. Ussachevsky began with a combination of "real" and electronic sounds as his sound source; these sounds were then subjected to a series of transformations to create the completed composition. At the beginning you may be able to identify the origin of some of the sounds. As the music progresses, it becomes almost impossible to identify the original sound source.

Composition for Synthesizer

by Milton Babbitt

This composition was created on a synthesizer. A synthesizer allows the composer to create the original sounds as well as their transformations directly on the machine. The composer can experiment on the synthesizer until he finds sound patterns he likes; these are then recorded on a tape recorder. For each sound that is included in the composition, the composer has to make several decisions. He must decide the frequency, tone color, duration, and the envelope. (The envelope is the way the sound begins and ends.) He also must indicate how each sound should progress to the next. The entire composition is created in this way. It can be heard by playing the tape, just as you might play a tape of music performed by conventional instruments.

Three Synchronisms for Instruments and Electronic Sounds

"No. 1 for Flute" by Mario Davidovsky

Some composers have explored combining electronic sounds with conventional instruments. In this kind of music the part for the instrument may be written in traditional notation. The electronic accompaniment is recorded on tape. The performer then plays the tape and synchronizes his performance with the taped sounds.

COMPOSE YOUR OWN ELECTRONIC MUSIC

Experimenting with a tape recorder will help you understand the basic process involved in composing electronic music. To develop your own electronic composition, follow these steps.

Select your "sound source." It might be your voice, a musical instrument, or a natural sound. Record it on tape.

Transform the original sound in various ways. Play the original tape at different speeds, and record the resulting sounds on a second tape recorder.

Then replay this tape at different speeds.

Make a "tape loop" by splicing two ends of your tape together in a circle; turn the tape upside down and play the sound backwards.

Play two sound patterns on two different recorders at different speeds; record the combination on a third tape recorder.

As you experiment, you will find other ways of transforming your sounds. When you have experimented with several ways, plan your composition; record the series of sounds to make the final tape.

Cindy

Southern Banjo Tune
Arranged by Kurt Miller
Traditional Words

Girls
Verse 1.

I went to see my, went to see my pret-ty Cin-dy gal, I

Boys

I went to see my, went to see my pret-ty Cin-dy gal, oh, yes, I

have no nick - el; have no dime; I

wish I had a nick - el, I wish I had a dime, I

have no girl to love me all the time. Get a- long

wish I had a pret-ty girl to love me all the time. Please won't you

home. _____ Get a-long home. _____ Get a-long

go now, Cin-dy, get on home? Go now, Cin-dy, get on home!

home. _____ I'll mar-ry you some-day.

Go now, Cin-dy, get on home, I'll mar-ry you some-day.

Verse 2.

I wish I had a nee-dle, as fine as I could

Loo, _____ Loo, _____

sew. I'd sew my-self to his coat-tail and

_____ Loo, _____

195

down the road we'd go. Home,____

Down the road we'd go. Get a-long home, Cin-dy, Cin-dy, get a-long

Home,____

home, Cin-dy, Cin-dy; Get a-long home, Cin-dy,

I'll mar-ry you some-day.____ I'll

Cin-dy, I'll mar-ry you some-day.____ I'll

mar-ry you, I'll mar-ry you, I'll mar-ry you some-

mar-ry you, I'll mar-ry you, I'll mar-ry you some-

day,____ Cin-dy?

day, now won't you go a-way, Cin-dy?

These Things Shall Be

Music by Thomas Williams
Words by John A. Symonds

Majestically

(Melody)

2. New arts of loft - ier mold,

1. These things shall be: a loft - ier race Than
2. New arts shall bloom of loft - ier mold, And

And mu - sic thrill the skies. Ev - ery

e'er the world hath known shall rise With
might - ier mu - sic thrill the skies, And

life shall be a song, a song,

flame of free - dom in their souls, And
ev - ery life shall be a song, When

When all earth is par - a - dise.

light of knowl - edge in their eyes.
all the earth is par - a - dise.

This Land Is Your Land

Words and Music
by Woody Guthrie

1. As I was walk - ing that rib - bon of high - way,
2. I've roamed and ram - bled and I fol-lowed my foot - steps
3. When the sun comes shin - ing, and I ___ was stroll - ing

I saw a - bove me that end - less sky - way,
To the spar - kling sands of her dia - mond des - erts,
And the wheat-fields wav - ing and the dust clouds roll - ing,

I saw be - low me that gold - en val - ley,
And all a - round me a voice came sound - ing,
As the fog was lift - ing, a voice was chant - ing,

This land was made for you and me. ___

198

Refrain

This land is your land, this land is my land,

From Cal - i - for - nia to the New York is - land,

From the red - wood for - est to the Gulf Stream wa - ters;

This land was made for you and me. _____

Music for Special Times

The Home Road

Words and Music
by John Alden Carpenter

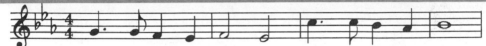

1. Sing a hymn of free - dom, Fling the ban - ner high!
2. In the qui - et hours ___ Of the star - ry night,

Sing the songs of Lib - er - ty, Songs that shall not die,
Dream the dreams of far - a - way, Home fires burn-ing bright,

Refrain

For the long, long road to Tip - pe - ra - ry Is the

road that leads me home, O'er hills and plains, By lakes and lanes, My

wood - lands! My corn - fields! My coun - try! My home!

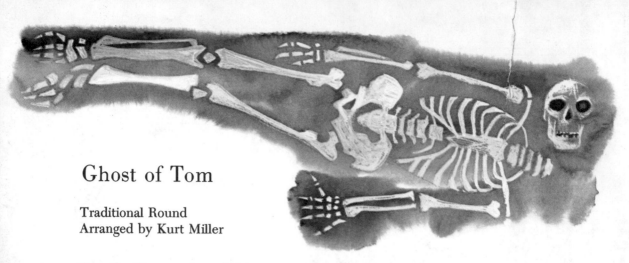

Ghost of Tom

Traditional Round
Arranged by Kurt Miller

Sing the first section of this song in unison. Then sing it as a round. When the last group finishes the round, everyone begins to sing the second section in two-part harmony.

Notice that the low part sings the same melody as the first four measures of the high part. There is one difference. Each note is twice as long. This is called **augmentation.** The note durations have been augmented or lengthened.

When you know the song, add a "spooky" accompaniment. Choose a melody pattern from the round, and play it over and over on the xylophone. Choose other percussion instruments to give special sound effects at appropriate times.

Plan an introduction and coda, using the instruments you played in the accompaniment.

Have you seen the ghost of Tom? Long white bones with the

flesh all gone. _____ Oh, _____

Would-n't it be chill-y with no skin on?

202

203

Thanksgiving Hymn

Netherlands Folk Song
Arranged by Edward Kremser
Words Translated by Theodore Baker

1. We gath - er to - geth - er to ask the Lord's bless - ing,
2. Be - side us to guide us, our God with us join - ing,
3. We all do ex - tol thee, thou lead - er tri - um - phant,

He chas - tens and has - tens his will to make known;
Or - dain - ing, main - tain - ing his king - dom di - vine,
And pray that thou still our de - fend - er will be.

The wick - ed op - press - ing, now cease __ from dis - tress - ing.
So from the be - gin - ning the fight __ we were win - ning;
Let thy con - gre - ga - tion es - cape __ trib - u - la - tion.

Sing prais - es to his name; __ he for - gets not his own.
Thou, Lord, wast at our side, __ all __ glo - ry be thine.
Thy name be ev - er praised! __ O __ Lord, make us free!

Haleluyoh

Jewish Folk Song

Ríu, Ríu, Chíu

Spanish Christmas Carol
Words Adapted

This carol is sung in free meter. As in all early music, this song originally had no bar lines. The bar lines added here indicate rhythmic groupings. There is no meter signature because not all measures contain the same number of beats.

Refrain

Rí - u, rí - u, chí - u, may you safe - ly guard us.

Nev - er shall we fear; God saves the meek a - mong us.

Fine

Nev - er shall we fear; God saves the meek a - mong us.

Verse

1. Man - y an - cient wise men told us of his com - ing.
2. We have al - ways prayed for one who'd come to save us.

Now it has come true; he is here and we have seen him.
Now our hearts are glad for the good - ness of our Lord. __

God came to the earth and brought glad - ness ev - ery - where.
Let us be to - geth - er and we will pre - sents share.

D.C. al Fine

Now all men are free for our Lord de - creed it so.
Ev - ery - where give thanks, sing His praise through - out the land.

Go Tell It on the
Mountain

Spiritual
Arranged by
Buryl Red

Brightly

Go, tell it on the moun-tain, O-ver the hills and

Go, tell it on the moun-tain, O-ver the hills and

ev - ery - where; Go, tell it on the

ev - ery - where; Go, tell it on the

207

moun - tain   That   Je - sus   Christ _ is   born!

moun - tain   That   Je - sus   Christ _ is ___ born!

1. While   shep - herds   kept   their   watch - ing   O'er
2. The   shep - herds   feared   and   trem - bled   When
3. Down   in   a   low - ly   man - ger   Our

1. Shep   -   herds   watched   o'er
2. Shep   -   herds   feared,   a -
3. Low   -   ly   man - ger

si - lent flocks by   night,   Be - hold through-out the
lo! a - bove the   earth,   Rang out   the   an - gel
hum - ble Christ was   born,   And God   sent   us   sal -

flocks   by   night, ___   Through - out
bove   the   earth ___   Cho - rus
Christ   was   born, ___   God   sent

Fum, Fum, Fum

Spanish Carol
English Words Adapted

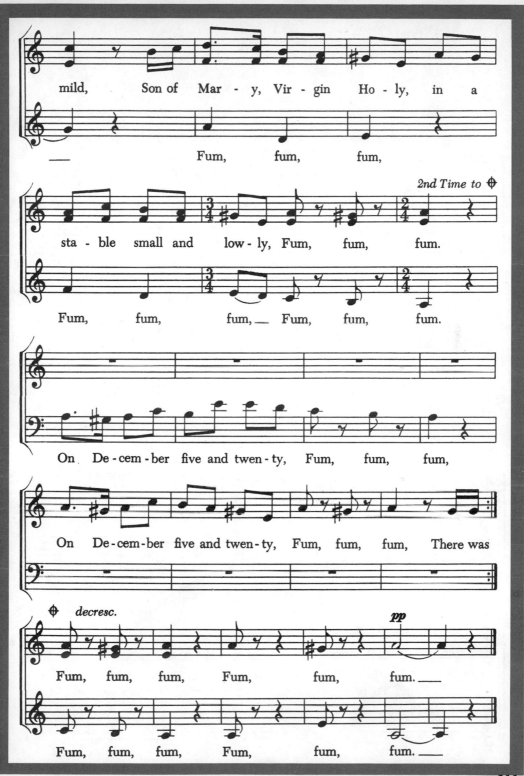

mild,   Son of Mar - y, Vir - gin Ho - ly, in a

— Fum,   fum,   fum,

2nd Time to ✛

sta - ble small and low - ly, Fum, fum, fum.

Fum,   fum,   fum, — Fum, fum, fum.

On De - cem - ber five and twen - ty, Fum, fum, fum,

On De - cem - ber five and twen - ty, Fum, fum, fum, There was

✛ *decresc.*   *pp*

Fum, fum, fum, Fum,   fum,   fum. —

Fum, fum, fum, Fum,   fum,   fum. —

Pat-A-Pan

French Carol
Arranged by Kurt Miller   Words Adapted by Kurt Miller

Pat - a - pat- a - pan, _____

_____ Tu - re - lu - re - ley, _____ Fife and

drum to - geth-er play on this joy - ous hol - i - day.

1. Bil - lie, bring your new red drum; Rob-bie, get your
2. There is mus - ic in the air, you can hear it

1. Bil - lie
2. Mus - ic

fife and come.
ev - ery - where.
Fife and drum to - geth - er

bring your drum.
ev - ery - where.
Rob -

play, Pat - a - pat - a - pan, Tu - re - lu - re - ley; Fife and

bie, your fife play; Fife and

drum to - geth - er play on this joy - ous hol - i - day.

Pat - a - pat - a - pan.

All Creatures of Our God and King

German Melody
Translated by William H. Draper
from a poem by St. Francis of Assisi

The influence of the church can be noted in the music of all parts of Europe.
The melody of this ancient hymn comes from Germany; the words are attrib-
uted to St. Francis of Assisi. Study the time line on page 66 to find out when
St. Francis lived.

beam, Thou sil - ver moon with soft - er

burn - ing sun with gold - en beam, Thou

gleam! Al - le - lu - ia! Al - le - lu - ia! Al - le -

sil - ver moon, Al - le - lu - ia! Al - le - lu - ia! Al - le -

f

lu - ia! Al - le - lu - ia! Al - le - lu - ia!

f

lu - ia! Al - le - lu - ia! Al - le - lu - ia!

Study the two voice parts of this song. When is the music written in **poly-phonic** style? When is it **homophonic**?

God of Our Fathers

Music by George W. Warren
Words by Daniel C. Roberts

1. God of our fa - thers,
2. Thy love di - vine hath
3. Re - fresh thy peo - ple

whose al - might - y hand
led us in the past;
on their toil - some way;

Leads forth in
In this free
Lead us from

beau - ty all the star - ry band
land by thee our lot is cast;
night to nev - er end - ing day;

Of shin - ing worlds in splen - dor through the skies,
Be thou our rul - er, guard - ian, guide, and stay,
Fill all our lives with love and grace di - vine,

Our grate - ful songs be - fore thy throne a - rise.
Thy word our law, thy paths our cho - sen way.
And glo - ry, laud, and praise be ev - er thine.

Let's Explore Art

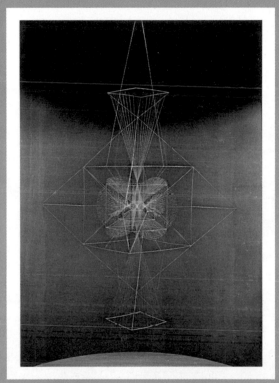

Variation Number 7: Full Moon 1949-1950, Richard Lippold (1915- , United States). Brass rods, nickel-chromium and stainless steel wire, 10' high. Collection: The Museum of Modern Art, New York. Mrs. Simon Guggenheim Fund.

The Blue Boy, Thomas Gainsborough (1727-1788, England). Oil on canvas.
Huntington Library and Art Gallery, San Marino, Calif.

218

Let's Explore Art

The visual arts, like music, help us to learn about different countries and periods of history. Every artist chooses from a variety of subjects and materials. The choices that he makes, along with any special techniques that he uses, can tell us much about the origin and purpose of his work.

The basic elements of visual art include space, form, line, texture, color, organization, and style. The use of **space** and creation of an illusion of space within a work are important concerns of the artist. The shapes and sizes of **forms** influence the balance and center of interest in a work. The direction, length, and thickness of **lines** contribute to the impression of movement and force.

Texture concerns the surface appearance of objects, or the way they feel to the touch. The use of **color** is important in almost all visual art. The way the artist combines space, form, line, texture, and color determines the organization of the work. **Style** in art is the result of the individuality of the artist, as well as the time and place in which he lives.

As you study works of art, think about how the basic elements are used. Notice the artist's choice of subject, material, and method. Relate the works to what you know of the time and place of their origin. Relate them to music you may know from the same time and region. Explore works of all types—drawing, painting, sculpture, architecture, the printed arts, and crafts.

Mont Sainte Victoire, 1904-1906, Paul Cézanne (1839-1906, France).
Watercolor. Philadelphia Museum of Art: George W. Elkins Collection.

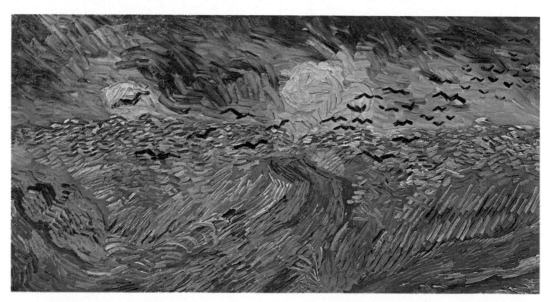

Crows over a Wheatfield, 1890, Vincent Van Gogh (1853-1890, Holland,
France). Oil. Stedelijk Museum, Amsterdam.

Guitar and Flowers, 1912, Juan Gris (1887-1927, Spain). Oil on canvas, 44⅓ x 27⅝". Collection: The Museum of Modern Art, New York. Bequest of Anna Erickson Levene in memory of her husband, Dr. Phoebus Aaron Theodor Levene.

The three paintings on these two pages have very strong and different styles. Look at each carefully and discover the method of painting in each style.

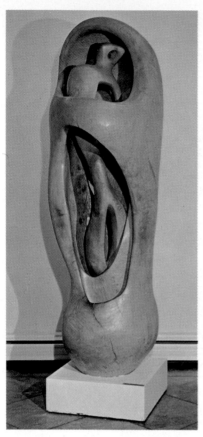

Internal and External Forms, Henry Moore (1898-   , England). Elmwood. Albright-Knox Art Gallery, Buffalo, New York. Consolidated Purchase Funds.

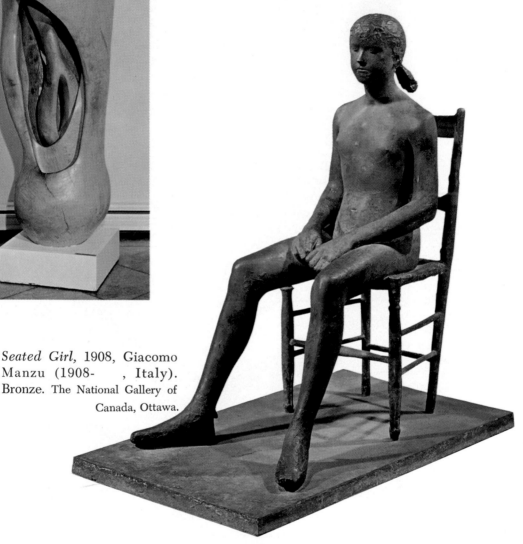

Seated Girl, 1908, Giacomo Manzu (1908-   , Italy). Bronze. The National Gallery of Canada, Ottawa.

From the art section of your book select three works that tell something about a place. Be ready to explain all that you can discover in each work about the place, its people, and life in a particular era.

Compare the subjects, materials, and methods of two sculptors in their works on this page.

222

Notice the time when da Vinci lived and think about the subject of his drawing. Do some reading about this artist and discover his wide interests and knowledge in that early time.

Create some art products of your own. Make drawings with pencil, charcoal, crayons, or some other material. Paint with watercolors, oils, or any material available to you. Create metal, wire, or string sculpture, carve in wood, soap, or stone, model in clay, or make prints. Use imagination and produce works that are distinctly your own.

Review the types of visual art listed in the last lines on page 219. Which types are represented in your book? Discover other types and other examples in museums and libraries.

Linear Construction in Space, Number 4, 1958, Naum Gabo (1890- , Russia, Germany, United States). Plastic and stainless steel, 40 x 21½″ high. Gift of the Friends of the Whitney Museum of American Art. Collection: Whitney Museum of American Art, New York.

Helicopter, Leonardo da Vinci (1459-1519, Italy). Sketch. Instituto di Francia, La Libreria dello Stato, Rome.

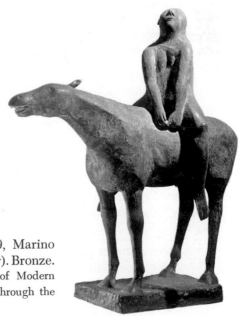

Horse and Rider, 1949, Marino Marini (1901- , Italy). Bronze. Collection: The Museum of Modern Art, New York. Acquired through the Lillie P. Bliss Bequest.

223

Performance of "La Contessa dei Numi" Given in Honor of the Birth of the Dauphin (Son of Louis XV) of France in Rome, November 27, 1729, in the Palace of Cardinal Melchior de Polignac, Detail. Giovanni Paolo Pannini (c. 1691-1765, Italy). Tempera. Louvre, Paris.

In the paintings on these two pages, how did each artist use the element of space? What important forms do you see in each? What textures? What is the chief character of the lines in each?

A great number of the world's art works have religious subjects. The painting by Michelangelo on the next page and the carved wood altarpiece on page 226 have to do with the Christian religion. In churches, museums, and books discover other art objects or paintings that have religious subjects.

The Holy Family, 1504, Michelangelo Buonarroti (1475-1546, Italy). Oil on wood. Uffizi, Florence.

Altar of Saint Mary, in the Herrgottskirche, Creglingen, Tilman
Riemenschneider (1460-1531, Germany). Wood.

Norwegian Stave Church, Borgund (Sogn) Norway.

Man, Woman and Child, Gustav Vigeland (1869-1943, Norway). Granite group in the Vigeland Sculpture Park, Oslo. Vigeland-Museet Oslo Kommunes Kunstsamlinger.

King Olger the Dane, 17th Century, Norwegian Chest. Painted wood.
Norsk Folkmuseum, Oslo.

Notice the country that produced these three works and the dates when they were created. How can the old church be called a work of art? What artistic beauty do you see in it? Consider the same questions as you look at the chest. What does the sculptor in the third work tell you about his subjects and his feeling for them?

View of Toledo, El Greco (1541-1614, Crete, Italy, Spain). Oil on canvas.
The Metropolitan Museum of Art, Bequest of Mrs. H. O. Havemeyer, 1929. The H. O.
Havemeyer Collection.

Mexican Pueblo, José Clemente Orozco (1883-1949, Mexico). Oil
From the collection of The Detroit Institute of Arts. Purchase, General Membership and
Donations Fund.

What do the paintings on these two pages tell you about the countries from
which they come? Talk about the special features of each artist's style.
Compare the use of the elements of space, forms, color, and organization.

Family Ride, Y. G. Srimati
(1935-   , India).
(1970 UNICEF Engagement Calendar),
UNICEF.

The Offering, Thai Nguyen Ba (1934-
, Viet-Nam).
(1970 UNICEF Engagement Calendar),
UNICEF.

Moonlight Revelry at the Dozo Sagami, Detail, 18th Century, Kitagawa
Utamaro (1753-1806, Japanese). Watercolor and mineral pigments on paper.
Courtesy of the Smithsonian Institution, Freer Gallery of Art, Washington, D. C.

Notice the three Asian countries and the periods of time from which the works
on these pages come. Observe each work and learn all that you can about the
people and their lives. How does the artist's use of the elements seem to fit
each subject? Relate these works to ideas and music in the section of your
book called "Music of the Pacific World."

Wonders of the Bush, contributed by Papa Ibra Tall of the Republic of Senegal to benefit UNICEF, the United Nations Children's Fund. Reproduced courtesy of UNICEF.

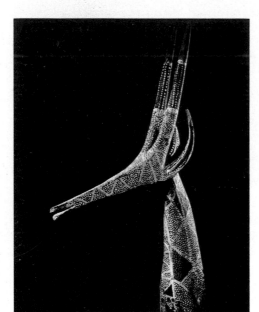

Kurumba Dance Headdress, in the form of an Antelope's head, from Aribinda upper Volta, West Africa. Painted wood.
Museum für Völkerkunde, Munich.

Bapende Female Mask from Kwango, Congo, 19th Century. Painted wood.
Museum für Völkerkunde, Munich.

Classified Index

233

Alphabetical Index of Music